The Wind Is My Mother

The Wind Is My Mother

THE LIFE AND TEACHINGS OF A NATIVE AMERICAN SHAMAN

Bear Heart

WITH MOLLY LARKIN

CLARKSON POTTER/PUBLISHERS
NEW YORK

This book is lovingly dedicated to my personal hero, who died in the Philippines on May 11, 1964, while in the service of our country—my son, Marc Nathan Williams.

B.H.

Copyright © 1996 by Bear Heart and Molly Larkin

Published by Clarkson N. Potter, Inc./Publishers, 201 East 50th Street, New York, New York 10022. Member of the Crown Publishing Group.

Random House, Inc. New York, Toronto, London, Sydney, Auckland

CLARKSON N. POTTER, POTTER, and colophon are trademarks of Crown Publishers, Inc.

Printed in the United States of America

Design by Debbie Glasserman

Library of Congress Cataloging-in-Publication Data
Bear Heart.
  The wind is my mother : the life and teachings of a Native American shaman / by Bear Heart with Molly Larkin. — 1st. ed.
    1. Bear Heart.   2. Creek Indians—Biography.   3. Shamans—Oklahoma—Biography.   4. Creek Indians—Religion.   5. Creek Indians—Rites and ceremonies.   I. Larkin, Molly.   II. Title.
E99.C9B43   1996   95-51335
299'.783—dc20   CIP

ISBN 0-517-702835

ACKNOWLEDGMENTS

IN THE YEARS THAT I'VE BEEN ALLOWED TO LIVE ON THIS planet, I've been most fortunate to have accumulated knowledge from various academic institutions as well as Native American teachings from individuals of various tribes. I also owe much of my knowledge to professional and nonprofessional individuals who are not Native American. If I were to list all the people who I would like to acknowledge, it would take up many pages of this book and I would regret omitting, overlooking, or forgetting someone who has helped me in my endeavors. For this reason, I mention only my immediate family: my wife, Edna; my daughter, Mari; and my five grandchildren, Robert, Stephanie, Angela, Caitlin, and Michelle, whose love and devotion continue to provide the inspiration that keeps me going on in this life. To all my relatives and friends, blood-kin as well as members of my extended family, please accept my love and gratitude for being a part of my life.

Mah-doh! [Thank you!]

B.H.

. . .

No goal in life is ever achieved alone. Even an endeavor as solitary as writing is accomplished only with much encouragement and guidance along the way.

First I thank my family for their unconditional love and support, especially during all the side roads I took to get here.

Marshall Thurber, Terry-Cole Whittaker, Jeff Alexander, and Warrior Spirit for teaching me that the only limits are the ones we set for ourselves—and that they are meant to be broken.

Our great agent, Jane Dystel, and wonderful editor, Carol Southern, for seeing the potential and nurturing this project to fruition.

Leonard Felder and Elinor Lenz for handing me the key to the door.

Larry Russ, Laura Stanton, and the partners of Russ, August and Kabat for being progressive employers who graciously tolerated my erratic work schedule while I wrote this book.

Glenn Schiffman, Christopher Gibson, Charles Cameron, Patricia Duncan, Terry Hekker, Patricia Kost, Gary Ruffin, and many, many friends for inspiration and advice.

And last, but far from least, thank you to Bear Heart and his elders before him for teaching me how to live.

M.L.

CONTENTS

INTRODUCTION
BY MOLLY LARKIN

In 1987, I was ready to die. In a twelve-month period, I had lost my business to an unscrupulous partner, filed for personal bankruptcy, my lover committed suicide, and, after rebounding into a relationship with an old boyfriend, I was left for a nineteen-year-old receptionist. My life was at its darkest point, and I had gone so far as to make a plan to end it. Then I met Bear Heart.

His words gave me hope, and my work with him since then has dramatically changed my life. It seemed only natural that a book on his teachings could inspire countless others just as he has helped and inspired me.

Looking back, I see my life as one long spiritual quest. My journey began with my wanting to be a nun in the eighth grade and changed course as I declared myself an atheist by my senior year of high school. I experimented with drugs in college, which was followed by twelve years of practicing meditation—two of them in an ashram. But neither chemicals nor Eastern religion brought me real peace of mind.

I gradually noticed, however, that when I was out in nature I felt a sense of serenity that years of struggling with meditation never gave me. Since Native American "religion" is based on a relationship with the earth and all living things, finding a Native American teacher willing to work with non-Indians—with me—seemed the clearest answer to finding peace and balance in my life.

Not long after my search for a Native teacher began, I met Cougar, a man of both white and Native American heritage, who I came to love very deeply. His suicide in 1987 was a devastating blow to me, but, as is often the case with tragedies, it proved to be a significant turning point in my life. Three weeks after Cougar's death, I traveled to Washington State for his memorial service and it was there that I met Bear Heart. Many people were grieving for Cougar, yet Bear Heart consoled them all with great warmth, depth, humor, and compassion—his ability to lift up our spirits seemed boundless.

Within a few months after I returned home to California, Bear Heart came to Los Angeles to conduct ceremonies and workshops. I attended them all and a friend, knowing of my deep depression, suggested I meet privately with him. I had no idea of what to expect, but something inside—perhaps intuition, or simply desperation—told me it was a good idea.

I spoke with Bear Heart about the past year and of my thoughts about wanting to end my life. During the thirty minutes I spent with him, he said one thing I'll never forget: "There are many kinds of death. It isn't necessary to leave the physical body in order to let a part of you die that doesn't serve you any longer. When you allow that to happen, you can be reborn into a new and better life." He also said he would like to put me on a vision quest, which I have since learned is in itself a form of spiritual rebirth.

I walked away from that meeting feeling there was hope; and since that time, my own spiritual work, along with the guidance and inspiration that Bear Heart has given me, has helped me to embrace life instead of run from it. I know I owe my life to the Great Spirit, but Bear Heart's gentle guidance led the way to that understanding.

There may be no culture within the United States as misunderstood as that of the Native American Indian. I have met people who thought Indians were extinct and others who assume all Native Americans are alcoholics living in poverty on reservations. Neither belief is correct. It is true that the population of today's Native American tribes is only a fraction of what it was before the Europeans claimed this continent and that 45 percent of all reservation Indians live below the poverty line. Life expectancy among reservation Indians is under fifty years of age and Native Americans have the highest infant-mortality rate of any group in the United States. And, for a variety of reasons both social and genetic, alcoholism is a great problem. Yet in spite of these obstacles, or perhaps because of them, many of the ceremonies and traditions practiced by Native Americans for centuries are still practiced today by their descendants.

The purpose of this book is not to encourage readers to seek out and participate in these ceremonies—the vast majority are neither available nor appropriate for most people. Much of Native American tradition has been lost forever and some is meant only to be passed from generation to generation of qualified medicine people. But there is much that we can still learn from Native American teachings, namely an approach to life and a way of relating to the earth and one another that is very different from that of Western society. Bear Heart is one of the few traditionally trained Native

American medicine men willing to share wisdom that we can all apply to our own lives.

Since our first meeting, I have sat in many ceremonies with Bear Heart, heard him speak innumerable times, and he has put me on five vision quests. The essence of his message, all of his words of wisdom that have so benefited me, are contained in the pages of this book.

The time I have spent absorbing these teachings and vision questing under Bear Heart's direction has helped me to know myself and my purpose. After growing up on advertisements, television shows, and movies designed to make me feel that I should be anyone except who I am, I no longer judge myself by my accomplishments, possessions, or by comparison to others. That very major transformation has brought me the serenity and peace of mind I had been seeking all my life, and it is my sincere hope that readers of this book will receive the same kind of inspiration from Bear Heart's words.

MOLLY LARKIN
Santa Monica, California

BOOK I

Initiation

1

TO WALK IN BEAUTY

WHEN I WAS THREE DAYS OLD, MY MOTHER TOOK ME TO A hilltop near our home and introduced me to the elements. First she introduced me to the Four Directions—East, South, West, and North. "I'm asking special blessings for this child. You surround our lives and keep us going. Please protect him and bring balance into his life."

Then she touched my tiny feet to this Mother Earth. "Dear Mother and Grandmother Earth, one day this child will walk, play, and run on you. I will try to teach him to have respect for you as he grows up. Wherever he may go, please be there supporting and taking care of him."

I was introduced to the sun. "Grandfather Sun, shine upon this child as he grows. Let every portion of his body be normal and strong in every way, not only physically but mentally. Wherever he is, surround him with your warm, loving energy. We know that there will be cloudy days in his life, but you are always constant and shining—please shine through to this child and keep him safe at all times."

She lifted me up to be embraced by the breeze as she spoke to the wind: "Please recognize this child. Sometimes you will blow strong, sometimes you'll be very gentle, but let him grow up knowing the value of your presence at all times as he lives upon this planet."

Next I was introduced to the water. "Water, we do not live without you. Water is life. I ask that this child never know thirst."

She put some ashes on my forehead, saying, "Fire, burn away the obstacles of life for this child. Make the way clear so that he will not stumble in walking a path of learning to love and respect all of life."

And that night, I was introduced to the full moon and the stars. These elements were to watch over me as I grew up, running around on the carpet of grass that my Mother and Grandmother Earth provided, breathing in the air that sustains life and flows within my body, taking away all the toxins as I exhaled.

I had a sense of belonging as I grew up because of my people's relationship with these elements, and I imagine that's why most of our people related to the environment so easily. We recognized a long time ago that there was life all around us—in the water, in the ground, in the vegetation. Children were introduced to the elements so that as we grew up, we were not looking down upon nature or looking up to nature. We felt a part of nature, on the same level. We respected each blade of grass, one leaf on a tree among many other leaves, everything.

My name is *Nokus Feke Ematha Tustanaki*—in your language it means "Bear Heart." I'm also known as Marcellus Williams and I was born in the state of Oklahoma in 1918.

My tribe is Muskogee, and we originally lived along the waterways of what is now Georgia and Alabama. The Europeans who eventually settled in that area didn't know of us as Muskogeans; they simply referred to us by our habitat,

"the Indians who live by the creeks." The name prevailed, so we are commonly known as Creek Indians, but in fact we are the Muskogee Nation.

In 1832, President Andrew Jackson signed an order to remove the native tribes from the southeastern United States, and it was then that the Muskogee were moved, along with the Chickasaws, Choctaws, and Cherokees. We walked all the way from our homes to "Indian Territory," which later became *Oklahoma*—that's a Choctaw word meaning "land of the red man." History has recorded that removal, but never once have the emotions been included in that record— what our people felt, what they had to leave behind, the hardships they had to endure.

The removal was forced; we were given no choice about it. When our people refused to leave their homes, soldiers would wrench a little child from the arms of his mother and bash his head against a tree, saying, "Go or we'll do likewise to all the children here." It's said that some of the soldiers took their sabers and slashed pregnant women down the front, cut them open. That's how our people were forced from their homeland.

Our people walked the entire distance, from sunup to sundown, herded along by soldiers on horseback. When our old people died along the way, there was no time allowed to give them a decent burial. Many of our loved ones were left in ravines, their bodies covered with leaves and brush because our people were forced to go on. It was a long walk, people got very tired, and the young children could not keep up with the adults, so people would carry them, handing them back and forth. But they didn't have the endurance to carry them all the time, so some children and their mothers had to be left behind. Those are just some of the hard-

ships our people endured on that walk, and out of those injustices came much lamenting and crying, so our people called it "The Trail of Tears."

I knew a man who went on that long walk as a child and he told me about it. At one point the people and the few horses they had were put on twelve dilapidated ferryboats to cross the Mississippi River. The ferry started sinking, so he grabbed his little sister, got on a horse, and headed for shore, all the while chased by soldiers who didn't want him riding. He was trying to hurry but the horse had to swim and was frightened from the commotion, so it was slow going. He had seen how brutal the soldiers could be and how the ferries were intentionally overloaded to make them sink, so he was making a break for his life. Someone came up behind him on another horse and grabbed his sister. "I was crying when I got to the shore," he said, "because I thought the soldiers took my sister, but I found out later one of my own people had helped me out."

Many of our people died crossing the Mississippi. When the survivors got across the river, many were soaked from swimming and it was freezing cold. One old woman, confused and exhausted from the ordeal, had no idea where she was—she thought she was back home and started giving instructions to the young ones. "Follow that trail and where it forks there's some dry sticks on the ground. Gather them and build a fire to warm the people." She remembered where to find firewood at home and, in her own mind, she thought she was there. Surely she wished she was there.

My great-great-grandmother was on that forced march. No matter what kind of weather, they had to go on and, walking in the snow without any shoes, her feet froze. Gangrene set in and her feet literally dropped from her legs. She's buried at Fort Gibson, Oklahoma, but there's no name

on those markers, just many, many crosses where our people died without recognition. I don't know where her grave is, but she's there among them.

Even after we were settled, that was not the end of our problems. Our children were taken from their parents and forced to go to boarding school, where they were not allowed to speak their native tongues—they had to speak English. The boarding school was a government school, so they had to march to and from class, make up their beds, do everything as if it were a military camp. This was forced upon our young children. Back then Native people took pride in their long hair, but the children had to have their hair cut short. Sometimes the administrators would just put a bowl over a child's head and cut around it, then they would laugh at the child.

Those are just some of the things that we endured. And yet today in our ceremonies, many of our people still pray for all mankind, whether they be black, yellow, red, or white. How is it possible, with a background like that among our people, to put out such love?

I grew up in the country three miles west of what is now Okemah, Oklahoma. The Creeks didn't live on reservations when they were settled in Indian Territory—each member of our tribe was given 180 acres by the government and my family lived on my mother's original allotment. My mother was nearing the end of her childbearing years when I came on the scene, so there was quite an age gap between my brothers and sisters and me. As a result, I had no close brothers to play, hunt, and get into all kinds of mischief with. I more or less grew up alone with my father and mother and got into mischief by myself.

My family thought I was going to be a singer at one time. My older brother even had a conservatory of music picked out for me, but because he had chosen it for me, I didn't want to go. I wanted to do my own choosing, do what I felt good about. I guess I was just a little rascal from a very early age, always trying to do my own thing and make up my own mind. I didn't want to be "little brother."

I attended a country school about a mile and a half from home and walked to school every day until I got a Shetland pony and rode. I used to ride horses all the time and loved to practice the trick riding I saw in the rodeo. Some days I'd come back from school standing up on the horse, who'd be just galloping away. My mother used to get after me. "You're going to fall off sometime." I just said, "I'll probably hurt myself, won't I?" Next time, I'd be riding backwards on the horse, or else I'd be galloping along and I'd jump off and hit the ground at a run, hanging on to the saddle horn. The momentum of that would lift me up and over to the other side of the horse. I saw the trick riders in the rodeos do something called the barrel roll, where they'd go under the horse and come up on the other side while the horse was still running. I practiced that out in the cotton field and hit the dirt many times, but eventually was able to do it.

All the farm kids worked a lot and were strong, but somehow I was able to get everybody else down and was considered the best wrestler in school. I used to run everywhere. I went out for track and practiced running through the corn field without touching a stalk, just darting back and forth. We lived three miles from Okemah, and when I went to town I'd jump off the porch and start running and never stop until I got there. Then I'd run back. One time my father found an iron pipe on the side of the road, which had fallen off a truck—probably on its way to one of the many oil fields being built around Okemah. The pipe just fit between the forks of two trees in front of our house, so we put it across and I tied a rope to it. I used to climb that rope with my hands, up and down, up and down.

In addition to giving those horses a lot of exercise, I would feed the hogs and chickens, tend the vegetable garden, milk the cow, and help my mother churn the milk into butter. There's never a good time to milk a cow. When I milked in summer the cow would swish its tail to get the flies away and hit me across the face. And no matter how cold it was, I'd still have to milk. I guess that's why the cow jumped over the moon one time—cold fingers!

We had a smokehouse where we cured hams and salted down pork and I remember bumblebees taking over the inside of that smokehouse one time. My dad took part of a roof shingle only as wide as his hand and, without a shirt on, walked into the smokehouse and shooed all the bumblebees out of there. I don't know why he didn't get stung because he was not a medicine man who had the power to protect himself. He just had a lot of guts—he was that kind of a man. I was quite in awe of what he did, so I found some wasps living in the hole of a tree and I stuck my finger in there and let them sting me, then I took the stingers out. It hurt for a while, kind of like getting a shot, but I got used to it. Sometimes I'd catch wasps and remove their stingers, then hold them and have wasps all over my hand. People didn't know they had no stingers, so they'd be really impressed. I guess I was about ten then.

I used to do crazy things. One day one of my school buddies wanted to trade sandwiches with me—my mom used to make me good meat sandwiches and my friend had only a bologna sandwich, but I traded with him anyway. I ate the bologna, but first I pulled off the skin and saved it. On the way home I cut off part of that skin, wet it down, then pasted it on my face so it looked like a long cut. When I got home, my mother was quite alarmed, crying out, "Oh, Chebon! [son]" and throwing her arms around me. When I pulled it off, she tried to scold me, but she was laughing too hard.

I was always told to come home before dark, but once, when I was around six or seven, I went to my neighbor's and got to playing with the neighbor boy. We had so much fun it was already dark when I got back. I went to my dad and said, "I'm sorry, I forgot your warning about being home before dark." He felt he had to back up his word, so he took a strap, folded it, and whacked me once. It wasn't too hard, but I felt bad that I had caused the father I adored so much to whip me, so I went to my room and cried myself to sleep.

A few days later I overheard my mother telling my older sister what had happened. She said that during the night my dad had cried, too, saying, "He came and told me and I still whipped him. I should have accepted his apology." He hardly slept that night, but he had to back up his words so that whenever he told me something I would listen. I think it hurt him more than it hurt me because I soon forgot about it. But it made me more cautious after that about overstepping the boundaries he set for me.

Even though he never gave up practicing our traditional ways, my dad was a Christian and very knowledgeable about the Bible. He'd often read a Scripture to me and then ask, "What do you think this means?" I was only nine years old then, but it made me think.

He read me the story of Noah sending a raven out from the ark to see if there was any land nearby, but the raven never came back. Then he sent a dove and the dove brought back an olive branch—that's why you always see the dove with an olive branch in its beak.

"That's a good story, but what do you think about that? What does it mean?"

I answered that there are two kinds of people. One kind, when asked to do something, will start out to do it and then go off and get interested in something else. They just go their own way. But then there are others who will think it is a privilege to be asked and they'll want to satisfy the person who asked them as well as themselves by working at the task until it's done—like the dove that came back.

He just nodded his head and never said "Right" or "Wrong," because he wasn't particularly interested in the answer, he just wanted to see my logic, how I was putting things together. That's what he was teaching.

My mother was a very dedicated Christian and most of her activity outside our home was centered around the all-Indian Greenleaf Baptist Church. She was one of the leaders of its women's organization and was kind of the backbone of the church, yet she would still work in some of our Indian ways. When the women of the church had a meeting, she had them fast before and during their meetings. Then they would eat together afterwards. She told me that fasting is a way of connecting to the Great Spirit—they fasted so that there would be no distraction from discussing the spiritual aspects of church activities.

I had also heard my parents say our people came to know things by fasting. When I was ten years old I still could not read Creek, even though I could speak it fluently, so I decided to fast and ask the Creator to help me learn to read. I took a Creek songbook out into the woods and looked closely at the words and letters as I sang. I did that several times, fasting from evening until two or three the next afternoon, and that's how I learned to read the Creek language. It was easy.

My mother was quite a talker, too, and wouldn't hesitate to address the men and let it be known what was needed in the church. She organized all kinds of things. She got the men to work picking cotton in the summer for some of the local farmers and donate their pay to the church. That was how the church could afford to feed all the visitors when they had big meetings.

At Christmastime she would organize a pecan sale to raise money to buy gifts for all the children of the church. After the last service on Christmas Eve a Santa Claus would come in with a sack of gifts on his back. An Indian Santa Claus who spoke Creek! It was a very jolly time.

PLANTING COTTON

My dad taught me to hitch a team of horses to a wagon and a plow when I was eight years old, and when I was ten he gave me two acres of land, saying, "If you want to plant something, go ahead. If you don't plant anything, let it grow wild. Maybe some rabbits will come, feed upon the plant life, and you can kill a rabbit to have something to eat. It's your choice." Don't let it sit idle, let it yield something—that's what he was teaching me.

So I planted two acres of cotton. It was good cotton, my very own, but I had to work it and do all the plowing. I knew which plowshare to use if I wanted to plow deeper and I knew how to plow between each row in an attempt to keep the weeds from coming up. I tied the lines to the horses behind my back; when I hit a root or a rock under the ground it would pull me forward and I'd hit the crossbar on the handles of the plow. Often I'd fall, but I'd dust myself off and keep going on. When the cotton grew up, I'd check each boll to see if there were any boll weevils in there, and if there were, we didn't have any spray, but at least we could pray. That's how I'd tend my two-acre cotton patch.

I did my best to excel in everything that I tried, but I definitely must say that I was not good at picking cotton. When I picked cotton from each boll, I'd pick it clean, and that takes a long time—it's stuck in there and you have to pull. The sharp, dried points of the cotton boll stick right under your fingernails and the edge of your fingers get all bloody. Some people could pick two rows of cotton at once—one cotton sack on their left side and another cotton sack on their right, ambidextrous, going down the line. It would take me about four times as long to finish one row of cotton, just one sack.

Because I had a lot of cousins living nearby, when it was time to pick the cotton, I hired them to pick it for me. I was the boss and we all picked the cotton. When each sack was full, I weighed it, recorded the weight next to the person's name, and dumped the cotton in the wagon. When we finished picking, I sold the cotton and paid them all off. I think the going rate for cotton at that time was about eight cents a pound.

Afterwards, one of my cousins drove me into town from Okemah to Okmulgee. I paid for the gas—it was just twenty-five cents a gallon in those days. When we got to Okmulgee, I bought a suede jacket and a new pair of work shoes. Boy, I came out the tallest man in that city because I'd bought something with money I earned with my own labor at ten years old.

Not long after that, my dad became very ill. He had been bedridden for some time when one day he called me over and said, "Son, I really hate to ask you to do this, but I'm going to ask if you would stay out of school for a while to help your mother around the house." I said yes. I was happy to get out of school anyway. People used to come over and pray for my dad or just visit with him, but as time went on and on, they quit coming, and so it was just my mother and myself.

The rest of the family helped us out. At the grocery store and gas station we just signed for our purchases and my older brother would pay for them. He wasn't a rich man, but he was well enough off financially to take care of us like that. Still, we did without a lot of things. There was no air conditioning back then, and even if there had been, we couldn't have afforded it. I built a brush arbor next to the porch of our house and in the summer we'd bring my dad's bed out there. I'd take the wagon to a spring about two and a half miles away and fill two barrels with water—then I'd come back and sprinkle around his bed and around the shade arbor. That was air conditioning in our day.

One hot Saturday afternoon in June, I was on my way to fill the barrels with water from the spring when, at the crossroads, I met two of my buddies from school going to town on horseback. I hadn't seen them for a while because I'd stayed out of school and I asked if they were going to take in the movie.

"Oh, no. We've been picking cotton and now we've got some money. Tomorrow is Father's Day, so we're going to get presents for our dads."

All I could say was, "Oh." I couldn't speak, so I went on. I wanted to get something for my dad, too, but I didn't have any money, didn't even have a penny in my pocket. That's why I couldn't talk—I was too choked up. After getting the water I came back home and did a lot of little extra things for my dad. I swept out the entire arbor, then I sprinkled on top of the willows that made up the shade for the arbor and I sprinkled around his bedside. I wished there was some way that I could make my dad happy on Father's Day, to honor him and give him something special. I thought that maybe if I did a real extra thing, something good would happen and I'd be able to get a present for my dad, but nothing happened. I didn't have much sleep during the night, thinking about it. Maybe some tears came, too.

Morning came and the first thing that I'd do each day was light the woodstove in the kitchen for my mother. Then I'd get a fresh bucket of water, go get the eggs, milk the cow, and feed the horses. That was my routine every morning. I got all that done and when I came back, my mother just about had breakfast ready for my dad.

At the last minute, as my mother was finishing making his breakfast, I had an inspiration. I ran into my room, took a page out of the old Chief tablet that I had used at school, and scribbled on it: "Dear Dad, you are the most wonderful dad in all this world. I love you very much. Happy Father's Day." Then I signed my name—that's all I could afford.

I handed him the tray with the note on it and he picked up the note and read it. When he got through reading it, he put his arms up and embraced me, and in that moment of embrace, I felt what a wonderful, blissful place awaits all of us when we cross over from this world. But until then, even a small portion of that greatness awaiting us can be experienced in a little embrace where love is expressed and manifested between parent and child.

I often think back over that Father's Day. Many times it carries me on as I look around at all the extended families that I have, reaching for something good and solid to take hold of, so that this world might be better for their being here. It's what enables me to do my work at the cost of criticism from my own people for sharing with non-Indians the philosophy, the love, the care of our ancestors. Coming into this world we didn't choose to be this particular color, from this particular culture. We are here, but for what purpose were we sent here? We try to find our role in life, and because of it, we can get glimpses of what it means to walk what we call the Spirit Road. And when we walk on that Spirit Road there is no Catholic, no Jewish, no Buddhist, no Indian way, or any special way. Universal love is gathered together on that one road. The caring and love that can generate from our hearts into the lives of others can carry us forward.

My mother was president of the women's organization of the Greenleaf Baptist Church for twenty-five consecutive years, and when she retired, they made her a lifetime honorary chairperson. During the honoring celebration they held in the church, an old man spoke, and in his speech, translated from our tribal language to English, he said, "During the years that you have supported this church with your love and acceptance of the Great Being in your life, you have made many tracks coming to this church. In time, beautiful flowers will grow in your footsteps, indicating a beautiful life lived with God."

I always remember that speech—to walk in beauty. Have a purpose, strive for its fulfillment. Strive to live in harmony and cultivate loyalty, belief, and faith. All of these are ingredients that give substance to a full life.

As a child I was taught, "Chebon, the way to attain the beauty in life is through harmony. Be in harmony with all things, but most important, be in harmony with yourself first. A lot will go on in your life, some good, some bad—people may argue and some will try to take control of your life— but that one word, *harmony,* will neutralize any problems and help your life to become beautiful."

Years later, I have people from all walks of life writing to me, and many of them end up saying, "Walk in beauty." I had that early in life, when I first started out. Our people walked in beauty.

2

A WELL-ROUNDED
EDUCATION

EARLY IN LIFE, MY PARENTS BEGAN TO TEACH ME WHAT THE word *respect* really means in practice. A first great lesson was respecting other people's rights and property; in fact, it was almost an unwritten law for all children to have that respect, especially for the elders.

If an elder came to the house, we immediately offered him a chair. Even though we might have been short on food, the first thing we did was prepare a meal for him. If we had nothing to eat, we'd at least offer him water. Maybe he was carrying a walking stick or hung his hat on the chair—the children were never to put on that floppy hat, make a horse out of that stick, or play around as kids usually do. If that stick and hat belonged to the old man, we didn't touch them, didn't even think about them. In that way they told us to respect the old man's belongings.

My parents told me, "When someone is talking, whether they're old people or not, children are not to butt in. You wait until they get through and then you can speak. If you see an old man coming along the pathway and there's room for only one person, stand aside and let him go on by, don't make the old one go around you. If you see him sitting out on a hot day, don't ask, 'Grampa, are you thirsty?' Just go ahead and get him some water, saying, 'Here, Grampa. Have some water.' He's going to thank you, and chances are, he's going to bless you. But don't do it for that. Do it out of respect for your elders."

When you have respect for the elders, it extends to everything else, including all of nature and its life forms.

The old people used to teach by telling stories—that's how we learned our legends. When elders came to visit, it almost always meant that, unless they lived nearby, they'd spend the night and go on the next day. At bedtime, the family made a palette for the children in the same room with the elders, and it was done for a reason. Understanding human nature, they knew that children like to eavesdrop. Knowing we were listening when we were supposed to have been asleep, the grown-ups told one another the legends of our tribe. They already knew the stories—they were telling them for our benefit. If we'd thought about it, it should have seemed odd for old people to be telling stories to one another. If they'd said to us, "I want you to listen to this story," we'd probably get bored, maybe forget about it, so in a way, they were great psychologists, because the thing that you're interested in most you're going to remember.

There was no television then, and those stories, told mostly in the wintertime, were our entertainment. The stories also held lessons as to what was appropriate and inappropriate behavior among our people, so the children were getting an education at the same time. I learned a lot of things when I was supposed to have been sleeping. One was the story of how the mourning dove came to be.

A little boy asked his grandfather, "Why does that dove have a sad song?" His grandfather told him, "It was something that happened a long time ago. A little dove's father and mother were killed by some humans, so he was raised by his grandmother, who loved him very much. As the dove got a little bigger, he started playing with other birds out in the forest and he'd stay out late. His grandmother said, 'I wish you wouldn't do that. It worries me for you to stay out late. Something might happen to you.' The dove said, 'All right. I won't stay out so late.' But then he met some other birds who played a game called gambling. I don't know what kind of gambling they did, but they played for acorns, walnuts, and hickory nuts and he'd go from one place to another to gamble. Once he got a whole lot of walnuts and didn't come back for several days.

"One day a messenger found the little dove and said, 'Your grandmother is very ill. You should come back.' 'Okay,' he said, 'after this game.' But after that game, he played another game, because he was winning. Two days passed and another messenger came. 'Your grandmother's very ill. We don't know whether she'll make it through the night.' 'All right,' he said. But he couldn't stop and still another day went by until all of a sudden he lost everything he had. He thought he had a lot of friends, but they had all left and he found himself alone.

"Then he began to think of his grandmother. He remembered how she loved him and took care of him, how she was always there for him when he was sick. 'Now I've let my grandmother down. I'll go straight home.' By the time he got there, his grandmother had died, so he told the people, 'From this day on, my song will be a sad song in mourning for my grandmother.' And that was the beginning of the mourning dove's song."

BECOMING A HUNTER

As much as we learned from our parents, Native American children received most of their education from their elders. *The boys received their training from either an uncle or grandfather, and the girls received theirs from an aunt or grandmother to learn the women's ways.*

My uncle Jonas Bear told me that a long time ago humans were able to talk to the animals. We were that friendly with them. They could understand us and we understood them, but at some point humans got into such a tight spot we had to take the life of certain animals for food and then we started getting sick. It turned out that various animals, even fish, were angry at us because we were eating them, so we started getting illnesses such as deer sickness and fish sickness.

A council of our people got together with all the four-leggeds, creatures of the waters, and those that fly in the air. We gave them offerings and told them, "My relatives, we have great need for you in order to live. When we hunt, we'll try to kill you quickly so that you will not suffer. In time, our bodies will lie down inside this Mother Earth and something will grow there so that our animal relatives can sustain their own lives. A cycle will be formed, an exchange, for the continuation of all life. In this way, we ask how to make our people well from the sickness you cause."

So the animals told us how to cure the illnesses and allowed us to hunt them because they knew that we were not killing them for sport; our need was to feed hungry people, and we used every part of the animal for our survival. As long as we kept our word, no sickness came.

That was the origin of how our people began to have

knowledge of curing different illnesses. And that's why our children were taught when they went out to hunt: "Never kill out of anger, nor for sport to see how many animals you can kill. Take just enough for survival and always be respectful of the four-leggeds. *If you must kill, present an offering and talk to the animal, explaining, 'I need you for my family.'*"

Children were not allowed to hunt until they became skilled with their weapons. We were taught the anatomical structure of each animal and exactly where to hit so it would die quickly and not suffer more than it had to. When we brought back the kill, even that was a ceremony. We gave an offering to the animal, honoring it and explaining why we took its life.

Young boys were taught never to eat their first kill—they were to give it to an elder. If you just killed and ate it yourself, that's about all you'd be able to do—you would not become a great hunter because you weren't showing much respect for the animal that you killed. But if you killed and made a sacrifice, giving that meat to others, then the motive for taking that life was based on generosity and respect. Those were the traits of a good hunter.

I was about eight when I killed my first squirrel. I used something similar to a slingshot and got pretty good with it. Before I shot the squirrel, I said, "My little brother, I'm going to take your life. I have an old aunt who has come to visit and she's not feeling too well—she's blind and can't do anything for herself at home. I understand that our four-legged relatives have medicine that can make humans feel better and I want this for my aunt. In time, when my body ceases to live and is put down into the ground, from it something will grow so that your people might eat and keep on living. That was the understanding between your people and mine. I will not let you suffer a long time, but I need you and the meat that you carry with you. I'm doing it out of love."

I killed that squirrel with my first shot. Before picking it up, I placed my hand over its head and made a circular motion, saying, "Mah-doh [Thank you]." The circular motion made with the hand symbolized the circle of life—humans being fed by animals, then animals feeding on the plant life after humans have been returned to the earth. A never-ending exchange.

Then I pulled the fur from the forelegs and buried it at the base of the tree where I'd found it to ensure that many more squirrels would be born to take the place of the one I killed. As I headed for home, I carried that squirrel carefully. Once we picked up the kill, we tried not to let it fall to the ground until we got back to our home because dragging it on the ground showed disrespect. The animal, even if involuntarily, gave itself to us—it was a gift.

I had a cousin who cooked for us and, knowing that I wasn't supposed to eat my first kill, when I got home, I gave the squirrel to her to cook for my aunt. I went back outside and was stooped over a wash basin washing my hands when all of a sudden, whack! My cousin whacked me with that squirrel, right on my rear end. I had forgotten all about it, but knew immediately what it meant. They did that with your first kill to make you a better hunter. She hit me on behalf of the squirrel, as if the squirrel itself was tagging me for killing him. Now we were even—I killed it but it hit me. It was a way of balancing everything out so that I wouldn't feel guilty about taking its life.

LEARNING HOW TO THINK

We didn't learn only about hunting and legends—children got a very well-rounded education from our elders. One elder sat down three of us boys who had just reached puberty and asked a theoretical question. "Suppose you were married and your wife and child were about to drown in the river. Which one would you save?"

One boy answered, "I'd save my wife."

"Why?" The elder wanted him to give a reason right there.

"The child is innocent and in its innocence it can go on. My wife and I could always have another child."

Then the elder turned to another. "What about you? Which one would you save?"

"I'd save my child."

"Why?"

"My wife and I would already have had our life together and the child needs a chance to live its life."

"What about you?"

I answered, "I love my child in a very special way and in another special way I love my wife. We might all drown together, but I'd try to save both."

None of these answers was right or wrong. What this elder was doing was teaching us how to think, set priorities, and give reasons why.

Jonas Bear once took me down to a pond and told me to look into it, asking, "What do you see?"

"I see my reflection."

"Put this stick in the water and stir up your reflection."

After I stirred it up, he asked, "Now what do you see?"

"My face is all distorted."

"Do you like what you see?"

"I know that it's not supposed to be that way."

"When you meet someone and you immediately dislike them, always remember you are seeing a reflection of yourself—there is something you don't like about yourself that you're not owning up to. When you see it in someone else, then you don't like that person, but in reality you are being displeased with yourself. Always remember that."

He was not a psychology teacher. He'd never even heard the word *psychology*.

Along with that teaching he said, "Some children are born deformed, perhaps without arms or legs, or disfigured on their face somehow. Maybe one side of the eye is totally missing, all covered up with flesh. It's our teaching, and we're very strict about it, to never stare at someone who has a deformity. Just look to one side and try not to keep looking at them. The reason is that whatever caused the deformity is going to think you like it so much that maybe it will cause your child to be born that way. Accept the child. They may look different, but they've got a heart just like you have; they have feelings just like you have. Play with them. Make them laugh if you can."

When a child was born deformed, our people said it was especially blessed—it would attract the attention of good people and create a lot of love. Not just sympathy, but love, so that it could grow into a useful life in spite of that deformity. So everyone seemed to pitch in and support the family as well as the child. That was part of our real strict teaching about not staring.

There were also many practical things I was taught. In our

way, when we're walking a long distance, or up a hill, we were told to imagine a ropelike cord coming out of our abdominal area. Picture the other end of that cord wrapped around a tree or a rock ahead of you and let it pull you like a wench pulling a car out of mud, then walk with your fingers kind of curved and as you swing along that cord is pulling you. After you reach the tree or rock, visualize wrapping the cord around some other object up ahead. After long walks you'll be walking at a steady pace, not too fast and not too slow, and you won't be huffing and puffing. You'll feel light and you can go a long distance that way.

My Heart Is Made Glad

I'm of two clans: my dad was of the Bear Clan and my mother was of the Wind Clan. So the Bear is my father and the Wind is my mother.

My father told me the story of how our clans had their beginning. A very thick fog settled over our people in the southern part of this continent for many, many days. The fog was so thick, it was hard to see even a hand in front of your face and our people didn't know what to do. They began to come together in groups—even the animals came and stood by our people. It lasted for several days, and then a strong wind came from the east and blew the fog away. When the fog cleared, one group had a bear with them, another had a deer, some had an alligator. So each group became the Bear Clan, Deer Clan, Alligator Clan, Bird Clan, and so on. The easternmost group had no birds or animals with them, but that's the direction the wind came from, so they became the Wind Clan.

One thing that used to really bug me was the fact that in

our tribe we had a tiger clan. I asked my elders, "Where in the world did we come across tigers so that we could have a tiger clan?" But I could never get a good answer, even from my elders. They just pointed toward the northwest and said, "We came from this direction."

As far as we can determine, the Muskogee migrated from the area known as Siberia and traveled across the Bering Strait. Our elders said, "We crossed the backbone of the universe [the Rocky Mountains] and continued to walk in a southeasterly direction until we came to the ocean, and there the old medicine people began to dive into the water." What they did down there I don't know, but when they came up, they said, "We'll lead the people inland and settle near the waterways because the medicine that we will use grows there." So they led the way inland to where Georgia and Alabama are now and that's where we settled.

I have read that there are tigers in Siberia. If our people came from there, then that's where they got the tiger clan, so I feel better about it now.

The Wind Clan are the orators of our tribe—they have beautiful, poetic ways of describing even a small thing, weaving pictures with their words. For example, they would never say, "I'm glad I came." That's no big deal. Instead they would say, "Today my heart is made glad I came."

I recall an old man talking about himself at a gathering. He was the chief in one of our villages and people came for a big dance that night in our ceremonial grounds. His speaker (interpreter) sat on his left and the old man told him how to voice what he had in his heart. The speaker stood up and said, "This is what I've been instructed to relay to you people. Our chief sits here, thinking back on the many gatherings like this held in times past. At that time he had elders he could talk with and things were good, but one by one they all left and today he's cloaked in the coat of loneliness. But by your coming he has opened that coat and his arms reach out to each one of you with gratitude, because you make things lively again around here. It puts joy in his heart to hear laughter, to hear voices, to hear little children playing. This is why these ceremonies were set forth—so that we could thrive and help one another make a future for our children. Today, he says, 'My heart is full because you helped to fill in those empty spaces.' "

That's the kind of speeches they made.

3

YOU DON'T ASK TO BE
A MEDICINE MAN

When I was a child our people rarely went to physicians when they were sick because the medicine men and women of our tribe had great knowledge of herbs and chants that could cure most any illness. I didn't really know too much about what they did, because when someone was being doctored by our medicine people, the children were sent somewhere else. The belief was that the illness taken out of a sick person could sometimes bounce over to those in their bloodline. So, for safety reasons, they used to keep us children occupied or tell us not to come around, not to bother the person doctoring, which of course made me even more curious about what was going on.

My mother had some kind of an illness when I was around eleven years old and she sent me to a relative who was a medicine man with instructions as to exactly what to say to him. She had fixed a bundle to give to him in exchange for his doctoring, and I brought it with me to his house. I told him about my mother's illness, and instead of coming home with me, he said, "I'll go ahead and fix the medicine and you can bring it back to her."

I sat out on the front porch while he went inside and I could hear him singing and using his blowpipe to blow into the medicine. When he was done he placed everything in a jar with a lid on it and handed it to me, telling me at what times she was to use the medicine. After I gave him the bundle from my mother, he shook my hand and I left.

I never did know the exact nature of her illness, only that she was feeling weak all over and couldn't do her work around the house and had to lie down a lot. I think she had diarrhea along with it, but she got better after that man fixed her medicine. That was my first real introduction to dealing with a medicine man in person, but I still was not allowed to ask questions about it and I didn't know that later on I would be learning some of those healing ways.

The Creek had about as many medicine women as men and their knowledge and abilities went far beyond the healing arts. In the old days, when our medicine people were not doctoring their patients or away on some quest, they would occasionally get together and take some time for themselves, meeting, drinking, and kind of letting off steam. I don't know where they got the liquor, because in those days it was illegal for Indians to drink, but they managed it somehow. They didn't do this all the time, just every now and then, as it was one of their ways of staying connected with the earth and humanity.

My mother told me about how they would show off in front of one another while they were drinking. As a child she saw one instance where one of them took a whisky bottle, said a chant, blew on the bottle, physically twisted the glass in his hands, and set it down—it was still glass, but it was as though it became something else in his hands, something that allowed itself to be reshaped. Another one took his belt off, blew on it, flung it on the floor, and it turned into a live snake. Those are just some of the things they did, kind of like boys showing off to one another—"I can do this." "That's nothing, watch this."

But they would also have occasion to perform such feats in the normal course of their responsibilities, such as preparing a delegate from the tribe to go to Washington. You may remember in the old westerns how the president of the United States was known to the Indian people as the "Great White Father." We could never understand why very few Indians were ever allowed to see the Great White Father in person—the representatives of the Great White Father could talk to the chief of the tribe, but our chief could never confront the head man of the white nation, there always had to be a go-between. Anyway, if a tribal delegate was going to Washington to speak on certain issues, the tribe would choose one of our medicine men to fix up the delegate for that trip in medicine ways.

In order to choose which medicine man would attend to the delegate, or perhaps even accompany him to Washington, they would all sit around in a circle, put a feather between them, and try out their powers. The medicine man who could fly that feather the highest got the job. When I was a small boy, I saw one instance where a medicine man made that feather move, then another made it stand on end. When it came to my mother's uncle, the feather just zipped straight up, several feet in the air, so he was the one designated.

Once the medicine man was chosen, he would fix an herb for the delegate to put in his mouth so that when he spoke he would be eloquent and clear in his presentation. At the same time that medicine would be fixed in such a way that his words would be heard by his audience as being worthy of consideration. Sometimes a medicine person would also fix face paint so that the delegate would be noticed out of a crowd of people and be looked upon with respect and favor. Those are just a few of the things that our medicine people used to do.

Medicine ways were the furthest thing from my mind when I was growing up, although I had always been interested in those able to help others who were in need. In addition to curing illnesses, there was a great deal of sorcery practiced in our tribe and I was always intrigued by the stories I heard and the things that I saw.

My father was an official interpreter for our tribe and he often interpreted for people wanting to buy mineral rights or land owned by our people. One of the people he interpreted for was a man named Anheuser from St. Louis. He was of the Anheuser-Busch beer family and he bought a lot of land from the Indians. One Christmas my dad came home with a big package and inside was a really nice overcoat that Mr. Anheuser had sent as a gift. I always remembered that— my father got paid to interpret but sometimes people would do something more to show their appreciation.

My father would also interpret when there was a court trial involving Creeks who didn't speak English. One of my mother's relatives had killed his wife—I was too small to understand what the argument had been about, but he was on trial in the white man's court, and every night I would listen when my father came home and told my mother what happened. One night my mother said, "I guess they'll send him up to the prison." My father answered, "I don't know about that. He knows a lot of medicine ways and I know he's going to use medicine during the trial." That's all he said. When the verdict came in, my relative got off.

When my dad first became sick, my older brother, who was not raised in the traditional ways, took him to a medical doctor who diagnosed him as having pernicious anemia. He had a tightness in his chest, arms, and legs, and was weak all over. Not too much was known about pernicious anemia at that time, but the doctor got pretty close to understanding it because he kept giving my dad liver extract. About the same time a relative of my mother's gave her some money, saying, "You might want to send for one of our medicine men to look after him." So that's what she did.

The medicine man came over and, after diagnosing the situation, shook his head and said, "This kind of illness is something new to our people. We've never experienced it before, so if you want to find someone else I'll understand. I can fix some medicine to make him feel better, but that's about all I can do." My mother went ahead and let him fix the medicine anyway, and there again I had to retreat, go look after the stock around the barn while he made the medicine.

After my father took that medicine, it seemed to loosen the tightness to where he could sit up in bed. But he was still weak. So it did help some, but, like the medicine man said, it was not a cure, it just made my dad feel better for a while.

It was around this same time that I was first told about witchcraft—how when a person is sick sorcerers will come around. We would sometimes see a dull glow of light off in the distance, and in our way it meant sorcerers who practiced the dark ways were coming. They could make themselves invisible and that light enabled them to see at night.

My dad was still lying out under the arbor and, knowing my father was ill, even though they hadn't caused his illness, the sorcerers wanted to get us to leave his bedside so they could get close enough to finish him off and suck out his heart— the heart of a dead person was their strength.

My mother's relatives told me, "When you see that light, go check on it, but don't go too far away from your father's bedside—that's what they want." My dad had a .45-caliber pistol, so when I saw that light I would start shooting in that direction, aiming up high so I wouldn't hit any animals. My relatives knew I did that, so when they came to visit at night they'd start singing real loud so I wouldn't shoot them. They were afraid of me.

We were warned that sorcerers could put an entire household to sleep from a distance, so we had medicine people make protection medicine and sprinkle it all around the arbor. When I saw anything unusual I would check on it, but I'd come right back to the arbor because as long as I stayed within it I was safe, and I'd sit up with my dad all night.

I had a cousin who on occasion stayed with us to help around the house and one night he came over and said he had learned a chant. If he sang it just before we went to sleep, we would wake up when the sorcerers came around. So he sang that chant and, feeling confident, we went to sleep on the porch instead of sitting up as we were supposed to. In the middle of the night, we woke up but we couldn't move our arms or legs. I guess something was missing from his chant. We were both awake and looking at each other, but that's about all we could do, so I started talking. "Those people who are coming will think we're all asleep."

"That's right. We really fooled them."

We kept talking like that and just by talking to each other we kept them away. We couldn't do anything else, but the sorcerers didn't know that.

My elders told me that before the white man came sorcery was not used on people—it was used to hunt animals when game was scarce. Once our people found an animal, they put it in a trancelike state, then they gave an offering and took its life so they would have food to eat. When our people were removed from Georgia and Alabama to Indian Territory, they didn't have the opportunity to hunt anymore, so they started using sorcery on humans. Some of our people had money that was given to them for the hardships they endured in having been moved to a new land. They didn't have banks, and if there were white men's banks around, they didn't trust them, so the sorcerer knew that they had money hidden somewhere around the house. He could put a whole household of people to sleep from a distance and open almost any door just by blowing on the lock. Then he'd go in and ask, "Where is your money?" and they would tell him.

Using a chant to shoot foreign objects into bodies used to be a very common occurrence, and it isn't only humans who can do it. The blue jay is a great protector and is very determined in protecting its own nest. One of my elders, Sam Butler, once observed a blue jay deal with a snake crawling up a tree toward his nest. The blue jay came around squawking and screaming and hollering and trying to divert that snake, but that snake kept going up the tree, getting close to that nest. So the blue jay flew way up high, then turned and dove straight at the snake and whizzed by. A moment later that snake toppled off and fell to the ground.

Sam said, "I began to wonder what happened, what that bird did to get that snake off the tree." So he went over to where the snake was still writhing around. Right in its head was one of the blue jay's feathers—shot straight through like an arrow. That's called shooting, and that's what that blue jay did to protect its young in the nest.

Sam went on to tell me that when there are blue jays around your house, they have come to protect and take care of you. The reason they're blue is that they were sent here by the Great Spirit. The sky is blue and it represents the Great Spirit above. The protection of the blue jay is one of the ways the Great Spirit acknowledges our presence here.

THE INVITATION

In our tribe, you didn't go out and say, "I want to be a medicine man." In fact, when you're young you're not even thinking about things like that. I certainly wasn't, but one day when I was eighteen years old, an old man came to see me.

We try not to let an old person come to us—we go see them. Maybe they need food, maybe they're sick or need to be attended to in some way. When an old person does come to you, there's usually a pretty good reason for them coming. They'll say, "I have something in mind," and they're going to tell you immediately. If they came with a certain purpose, they're not going to sit around and talk about politics and weather and about this and that all day long. We talk a lot, but we're not quite socializers just to pass the time or be pleasant.

So here's this old man, Daniel Beaver, who came to our home and the first thing we did was offer him something to eat. He sat there and ate and then he said to my mother, "I came to see your son here."

"All right. Go ahead and talk to him."

First he said, "Son, do you know me?"

"Yes."

"Do you also know what I do?"

"I know you help people."

"That's right. I've noticed you, I know your folks. I know where they come from, their clans. Upright people in every way. As I'm getting on in years, I find that perhaps I may not have too many days left. That I don't know. But of all the people I have known over the years through the medicine ways, I have been watching you, how you carry yourself, how you keep your word. I hear about you from other people. One day there was an old man who came to see your family. You saw him way down at the end of the road carrying his satchel and you ran all the way in that hot August afternoon. 'Grandpa, come in and eat with us. Let me carry your bag.' You carried it for him, you sat him down and gave him some food and water.

"I've heard a lot of things about you. Not only among our people but among the white people also. They all know you. In fact, the whole town of Okemah knows you—they always address you as 'Chief.' We know how you treat and care for other people. You may think nothing of those things, but it means a lot to us.

"What I have in mind is this—I have to turn my ways over to someone who's qualified. I've looked around in our own area and I haven't found anyone except you. Everywhere I look you keep coming back into my line of vision, so I know that you are the one to carry on. I would be honored if you would allow me to turn some of my medicine ways over to you."

In our tribe, we are taught early in life to be good recipients. When someone gives you something, whether a big thing or a small thing, our people say, "The Great Spirit doesn't look at size, only at how that gift is given." Non-Indians know how to give, but they don't always know how to receive things properly. They might say, "Aw, you shouldn't have . . . " or "Why?" They put a lot of little blocks up, because they're so used to giving, but not used to receiving. When someone gives to you, he wants to satisfy himself in some way by doing it, and if you say no, you hurt his feelings. That's what I learned from my parents.

I said, "Grandfather, you're going to give me something wonderful because, through your ways, you make people feel a little better, physically, mentally, or spiritually, so I would be the one honored to learn your ways. I will do my very best to take care of your gift in a good way."

That's how I got started with Daniel Beaver. Several weeks later another medicine man, Dave Lewis, came with the same thing in mind, so I have medicine ways coming to me from two lineages.

STARTING OUT

The first day I was to meet with Dave Lewis, I got there on time, but he didn't speak to me—he was going here and there, checking on his plants, tidying up his house, and making out like I wasn't even around. He had asked me to come, so I wondered why he was ignoring me. I kept looking at my watch and at one point I thought maybe I should leave, perhaps he had changed his mind.

After I thought about leaving I said to myself, "No, I'm going to wait this out, see how long it takes for him to notice me." He seemed to read my mind, because he immediately turned to me and said, "Now you have arrived." As soon as I made up my mind to stay, he felt I had arrived the way he wanted me to—any feelings of pride or that I was really somebody important had to go down the drain first. I had to empty all of that out of me to be able to learn something. When I reached that point he said, "Now you have arrived."

Before I learned about any of the chants or herbs, both my teachers spent the first few weeks in admonishment. Daniel told me, "I chose you because you're not a vengeful-type person. You're going to be in charge of powers that can hurt people. If someone slights you, you must not be tempted to use that power to get back at them. That's not always easy, because we're human beings—we have feelings, we have hurts. And yet at that time we can look to a Higher Being who has wisdom. We have small knowledge but He has knowledge beyond that, so let Him take care of acts against us. *To turn it over to Him, saying, 'You know better, please take care of this for me,' is actually the greatest warfare we can engage in.* It takes great character to be able to say that and mean it."

I was taught not to fix medicine for myself. I can ask someone to do it for me, but for myself I can't. If I do, that would be about all I could do from then on and I wouldn't be able to help anyone else. Even though it all comes from the same source, a medicine person goes in one of two directions: either working to help others, or working to help himself. Whichever way he chooses, he has to stay with that.

Along with the good medicine, I had to learn some of the ways of those who work with the dark side so that I would be able to help the victims of such acts. For instance, sorcerers can plant foreign objects in a person's body that will fester and cause an infection—the person can even die if not treated properly. I had to learn how such objects were implanted in order to know how to remove them. I learned those dark ways only for that reason, and that's why Dave and Daniel cautioned me a lot. In fact, I turned down one chant. I told Daniel Beaver, "If there's any way I don't have to learn to take a human life, it will be okay with me." He did teach me how to take the life of an animal, but I didn't want to be able to take the life of a human, or to make them sick. He honored my request, but later on I realized that humans are also animals, so the particular chant he taught me can take a human life. Daniel didn't tell me that, he let me figure it out for myself.

As he or she nears an age when it feels right to pass those things on, the Creek medicine person normally picks a minimum of four, but preferably seven apprentices. Each of the seven passes on to seven more—that way the medicine of that lineage goes on and on. One of my teachers passed on his ways to only two of us, at the time he selected me. He said he saw no others who were qualified.

In the beginning of my medicine training, there were many, many lessons and tests I had to go through. I had to learn about herbs, barks of trees, the inner parts of trees, leaves, and how to recognize them in each season, even in wintertime. Then I learned how to care for them after I got them. Some of them we never let touch the ground again—we'd pick it up and then we'd hang it under the eaves of the porch. If you ever went to a medicine person's house, there were many herbs hanging all around.

Then there are the chants we use. Some of our chants carry a power from way back in time. I consider myself an expert in our language, to a certain point, yet some of our medicine songs have words in them that are so old I have no idea what they mean. But they effect a result.

The medicine people of our tribe received their medicine through fasting and asking for guidance and help from Above. That's where a great deal of our medicine ways came from—during that time of fasting the Creator might reveal a chant or where to find a particular herb and give instruction on how to use it for treating different types of illness. They would go out and fast seven days to become a medicine person. The medical profession says a person can't last more than four days without food and water, but we like to do things cantankerous and contrary. Something that was handed down to us from a long time ago, we like to try it. And being of the Aries sign, when it says "Don't," that's an invitation to me. I had to go on many fasts to learn these medicine ways. I have fasted as long as seven days, but some of those old people stayed up there fourteen days without food or water in order to get these teachings. Those were very powerful medicine men.

IN THE RIVER AT MIDNIGHT

In addition to learning the chants and herbs, my training included many tests designed to test my character and faith. One of the first took place the time Dave Lewis had me stand in a river at midnight. He gave me a little white stone and said, "Swallow it. That's your staying power. Regardless of what happens, whatever you see, you stay put. But you still have a choice—if you can't stand it, you can swim away, but that's as far as your training is going to go; if you want to learn something, stay put. It's up to you."

I was determined to stay put even though I had no idea what might happen. I stood chest high in the waters of the South Canadian River that flow through Oklahoma as the clouds moved by, turning the night sky from dark to bright, then dark again. As I stood there looking upstream, I saw something just below the surface of the water going up and down. I could see little glimpses in the moonlight of something like a cow with little tiny bells on the tips of its horns approaching me. I don't know what the bells were made of, but they weren't brass or man-made—they were part of the cow itself, tiny bells making little tinkling sounds. It was coming right at me when all of a sudden it went down under the water and went right by as I stood there.

That wasn't all. Next I saw two giant arms with long fingers like tentacles coming toward me. At the last minute they passed me by and went on. Well, that wasn't so bad, so I still stood there. Then something kept bobbing up and down and a great snake with four heads came at me. That one really got close, but I held my ground and it went on by. As it passed me I heard a song, which came to me in such a way that I could repeat it after that. That's when Dave asked me to come on up and relate everything I saw.

"Did you hear anything?"

"I heard little bells."

"What else did you hear?"

"I heard a song."

"What was the song? Sing it."

I sang it for him and he said, "That snake gave you a song that you will be able to use in court situations. You can use it to fix tobacco to help our people be treated fairly."

I had to undergo many such tests in order to be open to receive the power of the songs. Some are so powerful that sometimes no herb is needed. To fix an earache, all we do is say a chant and blow on that ear. If someone cuts himself and is bleeding and can't get to a doctor for a tetanus shot, I take dirt, fix it with a chant, and put the dirt on the cut. First the pain goes away and then the bleeding stops and there will not be any infection. Once when I was spending the night with my grandson in Los Angeles, he was slicing up some cheese and included his finger in the slicing. I went outside, got some dirt and blew a little chant on it, then put the dirt on his finger. The bleeding stopped and the pain went away—in no time the wound was healed. It took a great deal to learn things like that.

I was taught how to suck poison out of a person's body. That took a lot of training. When I suck the poison out, I have to know how to keep from swallowing it myself. I have a protection song that I sing before I do it, but still, it's a very delicate procedure, and because of it Dave and Daniel told me, "Your teeth will go bad early," which they did. I tried to brush them really well, but the poison still weakened my teeth. Sometimes the sucking part would be so intense that my gums were sore for days afterwards. A lot of stuff is pulled out through sucking, but the smell is real bad and it can make you nauseated.

Then you've got to know how to close the opening from

which the poison came, because if you don't, the patient could get an infection. There's a chant you sing and then you blow on the wound. This closes it up so that no one would even know where it was.

Lying on an Anthill

These ways had to be tested for me to really know how to bring about results, and I always had the option to quit at any time if it got too rough for me. I was put on an anthill as part of my training, but not by Dave Lewis or Daniel Beaver. This teaching came from a Seminole man who was a clan relative of my father—the only name that I knew him by was *Nokus Ele'*, meaning Bear Paw.

Bear Paw didn't live near me, but when I was in my early twenties he came to visit, and said, "I'm getting sickly now and way up in age. I don't have much time left to spend with you, but I do want to put you through this one test because it will carry you through many situations where you will need to exert self-control."

He took me out to a huge anthill near our house in the country—it was about three feet across—and he told me to lie on it. All I had on was a pair of trunks and those big red ants crawled all over me. I wanted to brush them off, but I was afraid I might kill one, so I just lay there and let them crawl. The sun was so hot I had to close my eyes, and they even walked across my eyelids, yet never did one bite me. That was one of my tests, teaching me how to exert self-control. Bear Paw told me, "The Bible says, if someone slaps you on one cheek, turn the other cheek. It means that *you don't have to resort to force, you don't have to defend yourself*

when you have faith. If you didn't believe that, there would
have been resistance on your part and the ants would have
bitten you. This lesson in self-control is to condition you to
have acceptance and faith in your own life."

There are many, many instances in life when people tend
to get excited. A fire breaks out and they forget where the
exits are, and many people can get trampled because of panic.
Regardless of what happens, never hit the panic button.
Maybe there's an earthquake taking place—don't run out and
hurt yourself. Try to stay calm, see this thing through. It's a
part of nature, you are a part of nature, go with it. That's what
I learned lying on that anthill.

LITTLE BEAVER AND THE OLD SEER

When I started my training with Dave and Daniel, I was still
in high school. Having stayed out of school to help at home,
I graduated from high school in 1938, when I was twenty,
and the next year I went to Bacone College in Muskogee,
Oklahoma, where I majored in psychology. It wasn't too far
from home, so I was able to continue my studies with both
my teachers during college.

Dave and Daniel lived way out in the country and it was
hard for them to get around. Each time I went to see them
I took some groceries with me, then I would leave some cash
so they could get anything else they needed. There was no
talk about it whatsoever; it was an understood thing among
my people that we took care of elders in that way. When I
arrived, I was ready and we went right into the business of
their teaching me.

Our people are very patient. You think they've forgotten,

and then they say, "I want you to come over." I didn't study with them on a daily basis—maybe a week or two, or even a month, would go by between my sessions with them. That way I'd have time to digest what I'd learned and know it completely before they took me to the next step. That's why my training with these two teachers took fourteen years. I learned from both of them, alternating each month. One month I'd go to Daniel Beaver and then the next month I'd go to Dave Lewis.

The teacher who approached me first was Daniel Beaver. His Creek name was *Chote-ke E-chash-wah,* Little Beaver, and when he started teaching me he was around sixty years old. His leg had been amputated and he was blind from diabetes, but he still was alert in mind. Every time I visited him or went to him for more instructions, I gave him a gift of tobacco first thing—that's our way of showing respect. He accepted it and touched it all over like something very dear to him, then he'd put it aside.

Daniel always had Beechnut chewing tobacco in his mouth, and even when he was talking he'd expectorate into a nearby can, and then talk some more. He had a special tone to his voice, and once he started talking that tone never waivered. When he was through with one sentence, he would continue, not with a conjunction such as *and,* but with a sound like the grunt of a bear.

Daniel recalled stories and songs from memory and had the ability to paint pictures with words. Whether you understood the language or not, it was a joy just to listen to the sound of his voice as he went along making various sounds and tones. It was an old man's way of recalling from way back. He was telling me, "This is how it was."

He told me that there are some places on earth that make you feel as though you've been there before and there are other places where you're not very comfortable. Before this century, our elders had no knowledge of the magnetic pull between the north and south poles. Scientists have since established that migrating birds know which direction to take by following the magnetic pull from the earth, and our bodies also respond to these magnetic forces. If you're right on the magnetic alignment of north and south, you feel good. But if you're not on the magnetic lines that you're accustomed to—if, for example, mountains are hampering that pull in a certain way—you don't feel quite right. The elders understood this and had a way of aligning themselves to tolerate uncomfortable places when they traveled. They would stand facing either south or north and sing certain songs over and over until the people felt better.

Daniel also talked about children getting restless when the tribe came upon new land. Perhaps they were fleeing from the enemy and needed everything quiet. There are many different energies in a new land and they couldn't know all that might have gone on there before, or what entities might be present. Whenever the tribe arrived in a new camp, the medicine man had a blessing song he would sing so the energy would be calm and the children would sleep through the night without crying. Through their medicine ways, they put everything in a peaceful situation.

When I sponsor a vision quest and arrive on the land, I still use this way of blessing the entire area, surrounding the people who are going to be questing. That sets the stage for keeping in contact with the people who I send up the mountain to quest, and I maintain that contact until the last one comes back down.

It would have been very hard for Daniel to take me out and give me physical tests, so he focused on teaching me the chants and herbs. All my difficult physical tests came from my other teacher, *Ke-tha a-cho-le,* Old Seer, who was also known as Dave Lewis. He was skinny and wiry but very strong and he lived to be a very old man. Dave was the funny one, seeing humor in most everything. He would tell me to fast all day on Friday, even at school or work, then come to his house that night so he could work with me. That was pretty easy when I was in high school and college nearby, but after I graduated from college I was working in Oklahoma City and it was nearly two hundred miles to his house in Eufaula, Oklahoma, so he'd often be sound asleep by the time I got there. He'd leave the front door unlocked and a very dim light on so I could see my way around. He was hard of hearing and knocking didn't help, so I'd just open the door, go to his bedroom, and wake him up. He'd look up and say, "I ought to report you to the authorities for breaking into my home." He knew what I was there for, but that was his usual way of greeting me. He liked to tease a lot.

Most of our medicine men have a lot of humor, and Dave was really good at twisting things around. He didn't make fun of people—he was the kind of person ready to laugh at himself more than anyone else. He told me that in treating patients humor was the best way to break down any barriers or skepticism and help them view him as human and down to earth. He was very sensitive to the needs of the people, and he always told me that no matter how serious the situation, we must always maintain a balance between being a healer and being human. In that way we are able to empathize with a patient much better than if we take the attitude "They've come to see me because I'm a respected medicine man and I must be on my best behavior." Dave told me, "That's not the way to take care of the medicine. Be honest in dealing with people and let them see the humorous side of you as well as the serious side. The two go hand-in-hand, and if you make them laugh, they'll forget their troubles for a little while. Then you can explain to them what you're going to do with the medicine, how they've been affected by the illness, and how this medicine will offset that illness. Explain everything to the patient before making the medicine. That increases their belief that you know what you are doing, and that in itself is healing."

Do You Know This Chant?

Dave told me, "You're going to go through many, many fasts because *you can only retain when you're not full.* When you're full, distraction comes. You must be a clear channel in order to learn the songs and the chants. Sometimes I'll teach you a chant, later on I'll tell you what it means. We'll put many of these chants to the test to see if they have accepted you and will work for you."

In my second year with him, Dave sent me up on a mountain to fast for a vision and told me to come visit him on the fourth day of my fast. As soon as I got to his house he said, "Are you ready?" We didn't sit around and talk for a long time, although we could have—I could have listened to him all day because he made me laugh a lot.

He said, "The snake song that I taught you, do you know it?"

I said, "Well, you know how it is with knowledge. I can sing it, but I can't be certain whether I know it or not, because I haven't experienced anything except singing it."

"You gave the right answer. We're going to find out whether or not you know it."

We walked quite a ways from his house to a knoll, a little tiny hill with a tree on the far side. It was a hot and humid August day in Oklahoma and that tree afforded the only shade in the little gully on the other side of the knoll.

I didn't know what to expect. He had me give him my shoes and socks, then he pointed and said, "I'm going around to the other side of the hill. I'll be standing there waiting for you."

I kept looking at the little knoll in front of us and saw a rock, with an opening on the top that looked oily. I asked, "Is this part of an oil well, or what? I wonder if they drilled oil here." He just said, "Here I go," and he took off.

When he reached the other side he called to me, "Anytime you're ready, start that song. The fourth time through, start walking toward me. No matter what you see or hear, you keep singing and walking until you get to me."

So I started singing that snake song and as I began it for the fourth time I walked to the top of that knoll and then I knew why part of that rock was oily. I was looking at a rattlesnake den—the oily spot was where the snakes had been crawling back and forth. Down below was nothing but rattlesnakes lying in the shade from the tree in that hot afternoon. I was barefoot and I could hear each one of them rattling. I could see their fangs as their necks arched backward, ready to strike anytime, and there I was walking among them, singing for all I was worth. I kept singing and singing and I didn't stop.

I can't say that I wasn't afraid. I definitely had some tense moments and thoughts. But when you're singing a medicine song that you've been authorized to use, the power that you feel is hard to describe. There's a certain quality there that's not a matter of voice. Maybe you have a squeaky voice or it breaks in different directions when you hit a certain note. It's the feeling, the belief, the faith you have that this song came from way back, and you are now being entrusted with its care. It's something that's been preserved and taken care of by the elders of our tribe for a long time. Now it's being shared with you and you're trying your very best to stay at that same level of care and love. I knew that in time this song was going to help people—Dave would tell me how—but for the moment it was taking care of me.

I kept singing as I heard the snakes rattling their tails. Many of them were reared up, in position to strike, but I kept singing, and as I walked they backed up, making a path for me.

When I reached the other side, Dave, true to his word, was waiting for me. He pointed to the biggest snake in the group and said, "That's the grandfather. Pat his head four times and then come on up here with me." Still singing, I walked over to the snake, patted his head four times, and then went on up to where Dave was standing. Then I finished the song. Dave told me, "By singing that song four times, you put them in a trance. By patting the grandfather, you broke that trance so they could all go back to normal, to the power of the snake."

That was just one of many tests I had to go through. And knowing that song is why no one I send on vision quests has ever been bitten by a rattlesnake, even in rattlesnake season.

4

WRAPPED AROUND A TREE

OUR ELDERS DON'T TEACH IN THE CLASSROOM WAY—WITH first lesson, second lesson, third lesson. There's never a textbook with answers in the back. Many times they don't even explain themselves, so you have to figure a lot out yourself. We don't harass them with all kinds of questions: "Why? Tell me." We just accept that there's a purpose in what they do and say. A bit of the respect we have for our elders is never questioning them when they tell us something.

At the end of my first year of training, Dave Lewis again told me to fast for three days and then come see him on the fourth day of my fast. When I went to see him it was early morning and he took me up on a hill about a mile from his house. First thing I thought about were the ticks—you can get quite a severe illness from them. But I figured he knew what he was doing, so I went along with him.

He had already picked out a tree and said, "Wrap your legs around this tree, put your arms around it. You sit there like that, and I'll be back." Then he left, no more instruction than that.

I wanted to say, "Why? What time will you be back? What am I supposed to think about? What am I supposed to look for? What if I have to go to the bushes for something?" All of these things went through my mind, but I didn't voice them, and he didn't tell me anything. He just left me there. I had no idea when he would be back. Maybe nighttime. Maybe the next day. I wondered if he'd even be able to find me again! Still, I had to sit there wrapped around that tree, and the very first thing that came to me was that people would ask, "Did the tree talk to you?" And I'd say, "No, it barked."

So taking up these ways is not easy. I just sat there, wrapped around that tree, and began to think all kinds of things. Why should a grown man like me be sitting wrapped around a tree like this? I began to think of the many people I knew. What if they saw me wrapped around this tree? I had just graduated from high school, where I was voted the most promising student. What if they saw me now? "This one we thought would go a long ways up the ladder, and look at him now, wrapped around a tree."

Freud made a marvelous statement I'll always remember. A group of psychiatrists were trying to figure out the symbolism in some behavior and were analyzing it from every angle. Freud, who was a cigar smoker, just kept smoking away and said, "Sometimes a cigar is just a cigar."

Sometimes we overcomplicate things—they don't have to imply this or imply that. And as I began to think of that, I understood what Dave was trying to teach me without telling me. He was teaching me to work through my own pride, my own ego, my own self-importance. *I began to see that, when it comes right down to it, we are nothing until that nothing becomes so dedicated that it is like a vessel through which good things can move, an instrument for receiving knowledge and sharing it with others who might be in need.* You might think you're macho this and macho that, but what is that flesh worth? Not so much. It's what's inside that flesh that counts.

"Okay, that's what he wants me to work through. I'll sit here as long as he wants me to. I surrender to it."

After that acceptance, communication came. A tree cannot talk, but the Creator can communicate to us through any means—a bird, an animal, even a blade of grass. The type of communication that was coming to me came as thoughts and concepts, and I had no answers for the questions that I had.

First came not really a question but more of a statement about me: "So you think you know a lot of things?" I couldn't say anything, I just sat there. Besides, it would look silly, me talking to a tree. "Don't you know that the only thing you can say you actually know is that which you have experienced? Other than that, it's hearsay." Immediately, I thought about all those books in the library. Mathematics, physics, philosophy, psychology books, then books on sociology, anthropology, human behavior in the various cultures, in our modern society. A whole flood of ideas kept flowing through my mind—a whole library's worth of books. And the tree seemed to know my thoughts: "Yeah, you've read a lot of books. But it's someone else's thoughts and experiences in those books. To you it's hearsay, because you haven't experienced it. You don't know it, you only know something about it."

You can take a course in child development and think you're prepared for parenthood, but until you have a child of your own, what you've been taught doesn't mean a thing to you. So it comes back to our old teaching: *Never claim to know anything until you have experienced it yourself.* This doesn't mean you quit going to school and reading. Take all kinds of courses and read whatever you want to stimulate your potential. But you can't really say you know it when it's somebody else's experience you're studying. Go out and do it yourself and then you can say you know it.

So that's what he had wanted me to learn wrapped around that tree. Someone always given to trying to explain things might want to analyze the whole process, but I just left it the way it was, because to me it was meaningful to experience that lesson. I didn't catch it at first, but the lesson was right there. I had to toss my exaggerated self-importance out the window, I had to work through my pride to become just a human being.

At sundown, Dave finally came back. "Okay, you can let go now. I want you to learn to be like that tree. If that tree could only talk, it would tell us many things. When you're learning something, don't be yakking away. Learn to listen. Listen to the wind. If you're walking along and a covey of birds suddenly flies up in the air, stop. Something disturbed them. What was that something? Another animal? Another human being?" So the rest of that evening and way into the night he talked to me about the importance of learning to observe.

When we perceive any situation, whether it's an activity, a sport, a fight, or anything else, it's important to be able to observe without getting emotionally involved. When you see someone in great pain, your emotions may want to jump in so you can both have a good cry together—someone who cries with them might help a little, but very little. You can be of greater help if you are strong enough to lift that person's spirits up and not allow your emotions to get in the way. It's called *empathy*—you put your mind in that person's situation, but only your mind, while you stand in a safe place and try to bring that person to the same point of safety you are at.

There are many, many situations where you could allow your emotions to take over, but you would not be of much help if you did. You can go through the children's ward in a hospital where some children are all bandaged up, some might be in pain, and they will look to you with eyes full of hope that say, "Can you help me?" You look down feeling helpless, but even then you cannot allow your emotions to take over. You can be of more use to that child by just observing what he really seems to need and tenderly trying to give him courage and allay some of the fears and pain the child is feeling.

By standing aside, you can lend help, strength, and hope. Contact the One you go to with your own problems and ask if He might intervene at this time. "If at all possible, touch this child with Your healing hands, and if it's within Your will, please let this child be free from pain and begin to smile and enjoy life."

You yourself might want to cry when you see this situation, but to be of help you must become passive. To learn how to observe without becoming overwhelmed with emotions, you can do deep breathing—visualize that you are breathing in power from On High to bring you strength. You're not throwing your emotions out, you're not repressing them, they're still there, but you want to be strong enough to do some good for yourself as well as for others. After you breathe in strength, exhale the desire to go to pieces and cry. It's not going to make you cold or insensitive. It's going to help you learn to eventually control your own emotions so you can be of some help.

One of the most difficult parts of my training was learning to observe without judgment and without getting emotionally in-

volved—but that's the way you can better dispense your own power in ways that can truly help people.

Several days later, Dave had me spend an entire day doing nothing but observing from early morning to evening. I had to sit in a field all day long without moving my body—he told me just to move my eyes very slowly from side to side. What was I observing? What direction is the wind coming from? Does that cloud seem to contain any large amounts of moisture? Is it dark on the underside and light on top? If so, perhaps it's going to rain. If you see birds flying, are they circling or going in a straight line? Are they water birds flying to where there might be some water? If you're looking for water, perhaps you should head in that direction. There didn't have to be any particular significance to all the things I observed—the point was to not let anything escape my awareness, to master the difference between looking and seeing.

When you see any kind of a movement, don't turn your head quickly, just move your eyes slowly to one side. If you turn your head too quickly, the little animal or bird sitting on a tree limb is going to fly away. If you are motionless, they feel that you are not harmful—they accept you and come in close.

There are many aspects to observation that I wasn't aware of. I discovered that the peripheral part of your viewing space can catch movement more readily than looking straight ahead. You also listen for the sounds of the area. Did you hear a cow? Did it have a bell, was it lowing? Did you hear a horse snort? If you can register in your mind all the sounds common to your area, you can immediately pick up on anything unusual.

You can also apply these observation skills in the city, where it may be even more important to stay alert. As you walk down the street, observe from one corner to the other side of the street. Is it safe? Are there any people or situations that look dangerous to you? *Being aware of everything going on around you can save your life.*

I went out to the field on my own many times after that first time because I felt I had missed things and wasn't satisfied with my own performance. Dave didn't tell me to go back— he had started me off, but I continued on my own.

I used to go to the zoo and stare at the tigers. A tiger would look at me and I'd look back at him. I don't know how long I'd stand there, but I was determined not to look away first. I kept looking until the tiger finally looked away. I guess the barrier between us gave me some kind of confidence, but at the same time I felt I was making eye contact with a hostile animal—he represented that to me. From there I'd go to a lion and do the same thing. I had a lot of fun doing that, and no one could tell what I was doing, it just looked like I was standing there watching the animals.

Eventually I gave the tiger commands, not verbally, but in my mind. I would project the thought "Turn away. Turn away right now. Turn." He was very stubborn, but he would eventually turn. I kept doing it until the time it took him to turn away got shorter and shorter. I got training in using the power of my mind like that. I did this on my own in my late twenties—neither Dave nor Daniel suggested it.

We can apply observation to almost any walk of life. I used to teach salesmanship to handicapped people at Goodwill Industries. I would give them an orange and ask them to describe it to me and invariably all they would say was that it was orange in color and round.

"What else can you see on it?"

"That's about all."

"Your observation is very limited. You can tell where it had hung to a stem on the limb. You can even see the pores on the skin and certain streaks and discolorations. Learn to observe. What do you know about your product? What size is it? How heavy is it? What does it do? What is its capacity?"

They thought they had seen all they could, and yet as they kept trying, they could come up with more. As time went on, they were able to do much more selling. What helped me teach them was not going to a school for salesmanship. I learned just by observing out there in the country in Oklahoma and I taught them to do it, too.

If you don't think observation is all that hard, try to sit still for twenty minutes. If your nose itches, don't scratch it. If your leg cramps, don't stretch it. These are some of the things you have to contend with in observation. It's a far-reaching training that enables you to take in a whole situation in seconds.

The benefits of observation can manifest in all sorts of surprising ways. I started Fancy Dancing when I was in high school. Today, children start out real young if they're going to be serious athletes or dancers, but I got a late start. Fancy Dancing started with Buffalo Bill's Wild West Show around the end of the nineteenth century. Buffalo Bill wanted Indians to dance as part of the show, but it wasn't appropriate for the Indians to perform their ceremonial dances for entertainment, so, as a result, Fancy Dancing was created. It's a very beautiful and energetic type of dancing and the dancers wear elaborate costumes covered with feathers, bustles, and bells.

I did the War Dance and Fancy Dancing in the summertime and that took quite a bit of stamina, especially if you were in contention for first place and you had to dance over and over again, sometimes in hot weather. I had good endurance because I'd always been a runner, but much of my skill at dancing came from my powers of observation.

In dance contests you had to stop with both feet on the ground when the song ended, and if you didn't, you were disqualified. Most songs had predictable endings—when the song is going to end, there's a certain beat to indicate they're getting to the last phrase of that song and you're all set for it. But at intertribal gatherings, the Ponca tribe had what were called "trick songs"—they would be singing along and stop abruptly without any warning. It wasn't used all the time, but a trick song was a good way to get a lot of dancers disqualified all at once.

Because of my training in observation, I was usually able to anticipate when the trick song would end, so I was rarely disqualified. Dancers generate a certain rapport with the vibration of the drum and the singing, and while I was feeling the songs, I was able to detect something from the singers that told me the song was about to end. I have no other way of explaining how I knew that it was going to end other than to say that I had a rapport that put me in tune with the drum and the singers. I would stop just in time. That's how I kept winning contests over dancers who'd been dancing a lot longer than me, until in 1938. I won the National Fancy War Dancing Championship of the World and got a chance to perform at Madison Square Garden.

After college I went into the army, where I taught hand-to-hand combat—how to maim a person, how to disarm a person coming at you with a gun or knife, how to make killing blows. It was a fight for survival, a fight to kill. All in all, I didn't feel too good about some of the things I had to teach, but when I made the vow to protect our country at all costs, it included that. Maybe with a gun it might have been different—you're distanced from your victim—but hand-to-hand didn't sit too well with me. So, even though I was good at it, I tried to find other ways to fit in. Eventually I had the opportunity to apply for Intelligence and I went through a battery of tests until it was narrowed down to five of us. For our last test we were to have an interview with the general. We all sat in the outer office waiting for our turn to go in one by one. I was next to last to go in.

"Tell me how many pieces of furniture in the outer office."

I told him right away.

"Where was the desk?"

I told him, as well as where the chair was.

"Anything on the desk other than paperwork?"

"Yes, there were some dried-up dandelions in the pot on the right-hand corner."

"Was there anything on the walls?"

"Yes, two pictures. One was of Washington and it needed straightening up, sir."

"Okay. Next."

That was our test—whether we observed anything out there. I was the only one of the five to be chosen.

That is one of the great teachings I received from sitting wrapped around a tree in Oklahoma, being taught by a man who I don't believe went beyond seventh grade in school. He said, "It's one thing to live a long time—it's another thing to learn something in that space of time. *You've been given the gift of life—don't just become an old man, learn something.*"

COMMUNICATION FROM THE HEART

Daniel Beaver was an old man, an elder of our tribe, yet I don't think he ever went beyond a fifty-mile radius from his home during his entire lifetime. By the time I was twenty-four, I'd traveled all over the country and had studied psychology, sociology, cultural anthropology, and theology. I thought I knew a lot of things, but he was still teaching me. "One of these days you're going to have to talk to a banker, a white man who has control of money. Maybe you're going to have to borrow money."

In our culture, we don't always look a person in the eye when we speak to them—it's a kind of respect in our way to look either to the side or down. But he said, "Here, when you talk to him, he's going to be looking at you, and with that eye contact, he's going to be studying you. He'll most likely have gray or cold blue eyes. His face will look like a map with little blue lines and when he's upset it turns red and all those little maps come in the forefront like neon signs all over his face. Then you watch his neck and the veins there—one will stand out, almost ready to burst. There'll be a lot of tension. He's going to decide whether or not he can trust you with someone else's money, so his neck will be tight, and as it tightens up, his eyes will grow colder. He'll be very businesslike, but he'll be looking you over while you're talking. First he's going to look down at your shoes to see if you walk a lot. Are they scuffed? Are they shined? Are your heels run-down? Don't you have a car? Is it worth the gamble to loan this kind of a person any amount of money when he can't even handle his shoes?

"Then he'll look at your clothes. Are they clean? Have your trousers been slept in or are they pressed? He'll look at your fingernails. How well do you take care of yourself? He'll look from bottom on up while you're talking to him about why you need the money. He'll be listening, but he's more or less sizing you up. Then he'll begin to look at your eyes again. In the course of that conversation you have with the banker, he may even upset you. If he does, never raise your voice. If you have to answer, just keep it on a low key and keep talking to him.

"There's a kind of a 'lend me money' chant you can say under your breath, and this is how you must talk to that person. Say in your mind that you will communicate from your inner being to the inner being of that cold outer shell. Somewhere in there is a heart—it may be small, but you will have touched it. And then when you talk, look him straight in the eye—don't look down and don't slouch. Sit erect—you're a man, you're not begging, you're representing a cause. You have a good reason for wanting to borrow that money, so you look him straight in the eye when you talk to him.

"When you've got his full attention, that's when you breathe this chant. Then you talk some more about anything at all, but he's going to lend you the money. All of a sudden he'll say okay, and you'll walk out of that bank with it. But you pay it back. If you don't, whether anyone else knows about it or not, you're going to know and it will affect you—perhaps the next time you try to help someone, you'll forget your songs."

Like I said, Daniel had never been out in the great society, yet somehow he had practical insight into human behavior. What I had learned from psychology books was the same thing that he taught me.

A few years later, when I worked as a fund-raiser for Bacone College in Oklahoma, I was invited to speak to the third vice president of a major corporation. I got there at the scheduled time and began to think maybe he was an Indian—you get there at the appointed time and have to wait and wait. That's what I did, I waited and waited. Someone called me into another room and I waited some more in there. Then his personal secretary came in. "Mr. Sach will see you now. You will have approximately eight minutes."

I'm kind of on to the psychological stuff. Before you get to the carpet part, there's that tile floor that's supposed to make you self-conscious because it's so noisy as you walk on it, like going to your doom. And once you get there, the desk is wide, so as to say, "I'm important. You can't get close to me over here. You're a nobody. You keep yourself over there." That's what that desk is about. But it didn't matter, he was still a human being, and those words kept ringing inside my head—what this old man had taught me way back in Oklahoma, way back in the sticks, about insight.

He had a check already written out because he was a busy man, a "let's get this out of the way" type. Since it was a wide desk, I couldn't reach him. He tossed the check. "I suppose this is what you want." It fluttered around and finally landed, but I didn't really look at the amount. I looked straight at him and said, "Mr. Sach, I know you're a busy man and have many things to do. I appreciate the time you've taken even to ask me to come in. I don't want to take up any more of your time, so before I leave I'll return this check to you."

"Why?"

I never raised my voice, the old man had told me not to. "When you tossed that check to me, you placed me in the position of a beggar. But I'm representing a cause, and I believe in that cause very much. I don't want to put the institution in the same position that you placed me. So I'll return it, but you have my thanks anyway."

"Well, where is this school?"

Instead of eight minutes, I was there quite a while and he got a lesson on Indian education. It was the difference between $25 and $2,500, just by looking him in the eye and not ever raising my voice. I didn't even have to use the "lend me money" chant.

Insight. My teachers learned it, not through the university, but by communicating. That's how they came to understand life, behavior, response to stimuli. In our society today, we live in what some people call a "new age." It makes me smile many times because the things they do are not new. When our own people treated a patient, if something was wrong on one side of the body, they treated the opposite side. They received this knowledge from above. Today, scientists know that the left side of the brain controls the right side of the body and vice versa. But how did our elders know that? They never went to medical school to study anatomy. That insight came from communication.

The environment was our starting point in learning as much as we could from what was around us—the seasons, the things that grow, the animals, the birds, and various other life forms. Then we would begin the long process of trying to learn about that which is within ourselves. We didn't have any textbooks, we didn't have any great psychiatrists who lived years ago and presented theories in this and that. We had to rely on something else, and that was our senses. Rather than through scientific investigation, we sensed those things within and around us.

METHUSELAH

Our people learned to predict by observing the environment. They could read things in the rocks. What does moss on a rock have to tell us? Moss usually grows on the north side— the direction the wind comes from. If the moss is covering most of the north side of the rock or tree, you're going to have a hard winter. The south side will never have as much moss as the north side unless there's going to be a significant change in the weather, such as might be caused by a shift in the earth's orbit. Our Indian people didn't know about the orbit of our earth, but they knew that something could shift, causing tornadoes to be where they weren't heard of before. Those are some of the clues that helped our people know what kind of preparation to make before winter came. Our old people used to refer to the north as "the direction that causes our larder to go empty," meaning that it was always possible that what they had hunted and put in storage might not be sufficient—if the winter was very harsh, they could run out of food.

Observation of the land itself, the sky, and how the wind was shifting were all clues as to what kind of weather was brewing. We became so sensitive to the outdoors that we could almost smell rain or snow coming before the sky turned cloudy. It's a matter of becoming sensitive to the environment, and you don't become sensitive to it by reading the business section every day over a cup of coffee, or watching your favorite TV program. Today pollution also interferes with the ability to sense the weather changes. You turn on the news and the weatherman tells you what's going to take place, and a lot of time the weather, in spite of all their instruments, doesn't follow their prediction.

Some of our people could look into the stars and read them like a book. I never did know how they did it, but they made predictions from the stars and moon just as they did from looking on nature.

There was an old man I knew from my childhood. He was an old man when I first knew him, he was an old man while I was growing up, and he was still an old man after I became an adult. I have no idea how old he was, but I called him Methuselah. When I was about twelve years old I went over to his house and found him looking up in the night sky, so I asked, "What are you looking at?"

"See those stripes up there?"

I didn't see any stripes, but I lied and said yes. Then when I looked hard enough I saw them, so he'd made an honest boy out of me.

"By the time you get of age, you're going to be wearing the uniform of our country because there's going to be a great war."

I forgot about it until one cold winter night when, trying to huddle up as best as I could in a foxhole, those words came back to me, "You will wear the uniform of our country." It came true. He read in the stars years before that I would be involved in some way—he saw what looked like flag stripes in the sky and they were pointed at one another, indicating a war. People like Methuselah didn't pass themselves off as great psychics. They simply looked upon themselves as being sensitive to the things around them, without some fancy label attached to it.

When the film *Dances With Wolves* came out, someone asked me, "That was supposed to be authentic all the way through. What do you think?" I replied, "It was very authentic, with one exception. In the movie, Dunbar had to ride like hell to let the Indians know that the buffalo were coming. In fact, each tribe had a buffalo man who was responsible for locating buffalo. Even if the buffalo were a hundred miles away from their camp, the buffalo man would have known where they were."

Most tribes had seers like Methuselah who could foretell future events—their intuition was highly developed, or, as Native Americans like to say, they were sensitive. Some had fasted to be able to sense the presence of a particular animal spirit. The one who dealt with buffalo almost had to have that as a specialty, because buffalo were the staple of the entire tribe and very important. The buffalo man became so in tune with the buffalo that he knew how far away they were and in which direction. If the buffalo were real close, the tribe would have known it already and not have to be awakened in the middle of the night and told, "The buffalo are here." It makes good drama, but they would have already known.

Many Navajos were employed to lay rails for the old railroads. There's a story about a group of Navajos being told to lay rails on a curve, but they refused to do it. When the foreman asked why, they answered, "The train will turn over and hurt a lot of people."

"It says right here on the plan to lay it this way. It will be safe."

They argued, but the Indians still wouldn't work. Finally the chief engineer was called in and he looked at the plans. "Fellows, they're right. I made a mistake."

So that was their intuition and powers of observation at work. They were not engineers, but they knew the weight and speed of the train on that sharp turn would have caused a wreck.

To teach our young people how to get in touch with nature and their own intuition, our elders used to take them way out in the woods, blindfolded, and have them sit by a particular tree. "You stay here blindfolded until we come after you. Be with this tree, touch it, hug it, lean against it, stand by it. Learn something from it." After half a day or more, they would bring them back to camp, remove the blindfold, and say, "Go find your tree." After touching a lot of trees, they could find the one they had spent time with. Sometimes they didn't have to touch a lot of trees—those with highly developed intuition could go right to their tree. They seemed to be drawn to it.

That's how we began to connect. It's amazing what you feel from a tree. It can give us energy. When we take long hikes in wooded areas, we often put our fingertips on the ends of the cedar or the pine needles. Just standing there touching them, you're going to feel energy come to you. Trees are emitting energy all the time. Every needle of the tree, every leaf, is trying to make the atmosphere breathable for us. That's why my people have great respect for trees. The trees are our relatives—we call them "tall standing brothers."

I Will Walk Again

After fourteen years, there came a day when I finally got through with my training. When Daniel had given me all the instruction he could, he said, "Chebon, I have tried my very best to recall all that I have learned in life and share it with you. You're ready to go on your own now." Although I had permission to use the medicine at any time, I felt that as long as Daniel Beaver and Dave Lewis were alive, I didn't want to use it because people came to them for help and the donations they received were all they had to live on. It was known that I was studying with them and people would come to me for help, but I told them, "While my teachers are still living, I would appreciate it if you would ask one of them." By that time I was thirty-two years old and had a job with the Indian Affairs Commission, working for all the tribes in the state of Oklahoma, so I didn't have to rely on the medicine ways to make a living.

It went on like that until they finally realized what I was doing. They came to me separately, but both had essentially the same thing to say: "You should be using those songs and chants I gave you. That way, if you have any questions while I'm still around, you can come to me and we can talk it over. So it's all right if people come to you and ask for help. Go ahead and help them." Reluctantly I began to use the medicine ways. I didn't advertise because we don't operate like that—we don't even tell anyone that we know these things. The people in our tribe, by looking at us, can sense there's something special about us—by the way we wear a certain feather, the way we conduct ourselves, they know that we carry medicine.

I remember my last conversation with Daniel Beaver, after he told me he'd done his best and was turning everything over to me. He sat with his eyes closed for quite a while and just as I started to wonder if he had gone to sleep or into a diabetic coma, he opened his eyes and softly said, "Chebon, I'm very happy that I'm going to walk again." I didn't know what he meant, and I thought, "Is he talking about the time when he crosses over? That in some way he will be intact so he can physically walk again?" I didn't understand at the time. But I embraced him and shook his hand, with every intention of continuing to come back and tell him about my experiences, not to enhance myself as knowing something, but to show that what he had imparted was continuing. "What you taught me, I tried it that way and they're getting along all right now." But he died a few weeks later and I never got a chance to tell him.

Not too long after his death, I was called upon to help someone and it required medicine that had to be fixed after midnight. Some of these songs are meant to be sung only at certain times of the day and so I waited until after midnight to sing over a big bucket filled with water and herbs. This was a very long song, covering many, many facets of healing, because the ailment was quite severe, and after singing each stanza of the song, I had to blow four times into the water with a blowpipe.

I had just got through singing the chant and was ready to blow into that water when I heard Daniel right behind me—

he had a distinctive way of clearing his throat. Then it came to me, "Yes, he's walking again, this is what he meant—every time I take that medicine out and use it, he is walking again because that medicine, helping people, was his whole life." That's why I'm very happy that other people are being helped and I have a part in it. I'm walking this path and he's walking through me. In the preservation of what has been entrusted into my care, I'm representing my teachers and the medicine ways of my people.

And in turn, now I can sit on the side and watch the fruits of my labor, what I have invested in those I have taught. They're carrying on now while I'm still living here and can be a recipient of the love and prayers that they make for me. Those are some of the things that give me encouragement to keep going on regardless of how tired I may get or the obstacles I may face.

BOOK II

The Cure Lies Within You

5

WHOSE POWER IS IT?

THERE ARE TWO THINGS OUR MEDICINE PEOPLE ARE NEVER supposed to say of themselves. First, we don't call ourselves "medicine people." A lot of people like to do that, call themselves "medicine man" or "medicine woman," but to begin with, we don't make medicine. The medicine is already here—we just have certain knowledge that can put things together to bring about results. Second, we're never to call ourselves healers or take credit when a patient we work with gets better—we are merely helpers. There's only one healer and that's the One who created us. He's the only one who can heal.

Even M.D.s, the very best of physicians, no matter how plush their offices, are still "practicing physicians" because they don't know it all. As for healing, they don't heal—they just get things ready for healing to take place. They rely upon other powers to do the healing, whether they acknowledge it or not.

A man or a woman commonly referred to as a "medicine person" is someone who acquires knowledge enabling him to work with people so that help and healing can come from On High. As we dispense that knowledge, it has to be done in a certain way. We have to keep that sacred trust and take care of it responsibly. We're caretakers of sacred knowledge—that's all we are.

For a long time, our medicine people didn't talk about our medicine ways. For one thing, non-Indians would find some of the things we're able to accomplish hard to believe. For another thing, Indians have been accused of every imaginable crime because they didn't understand the laws of this land and they didn't want to make things worse for themselves by revealing powers non-Indians wouldn't understand.

The United States Government allotted the eastern part of what is now Oklahoma for the Indian people to settle in, but it wasn't long before the white ranchers came and ran their cattle over the lush, green pasturelands of Indian territory. When the Indians tried to drive them off, they were taken to the nearest civil court in Fort Smith, Arkansas— that's where Judge Roy Bean, "the hanging judge," had his court. Many of our Indian people were found guilty of cattle rustling when they were merely trying to get the cattle off land they legally owned. With things like that going on they didn't dare talk about medicine ways because they might even be charged with practicing medicine without a license, so they kept mum about it for a long time. It's only recently that we've begun to share some of our ways.

During my training, Dave Lewis explained to me that our people didn't understand the white man's laws and often didn't know they had done anything wrong until they landed in jail. Sometimes in court they agreed to certain statements, which made them seem more guilty than ever. So, to help our people be treated fairly in court situations, he told me how to use the song I learned during my test in the river as the four-headed snake passed me by.

Many years later, I had occasion to use that song. My nephew Jack had been arrested and charged with assault and battery when he was in the wrong place at the wrong time, trying to help a friend. The friend had gone to his ex-wife's apartment to see his four-year-old daughter. He found a big party in progress and the mother nowhere in sight, so he took the girl to Jack's apartment a few blocks away and said, "If your wife can look after my child, I'd like for you to go back to the party with me and wait for her mother to come home."

My nephew had been asleep, but he got dressed and they both headed for the apartment to wait for the mother to come home so they could talk to her about having left the child. Meanwhile, the mother had returned, found her daughter gone, and called the sheriff.

The sheriff showed up just as Jack and his friend approached the apartment. One of the people who knew Jack yelled, "Jack, run, they're going to kill you." When you're an Indian and frequently subject to harassment by roughnecks, you don't usually wait around to see what's going to happen. His buddy ran one way and Jack the other. He hadn't gotten too far when he felt someone grab him from behind, and not knowing it was a policeman, Jack spun around and knocked him to the ground. Jack fell at the same time and another deputy came up and arrested him for assault and battery of an officer.

Before Jack's trial, I used the song I learned in the river to fix tobacco and took it to the courthouse. No one ever saw me there because I used another chant to make myself invisible—the chant doesn't literally make you invisible, but it keeps people from noticing you. Early in the morning I spread tobacco around all the entrances of the courthouse while saying the names of the judge and prosecuting attorney as well as the sheriff and deputies. I fixed the doorways they'd be entering so when they walked through the door they were already subject to that medicine.

I sat through the whole proceeding—they still didn't notice me there. When the sheriff and his deputies got on the stand, they made mistakes and contradicted one another. When the prosecuting attorney got up, he spoke only two minutes and then sat down, which surprised even Jack's attorney. "You through?" he asked. That was the easiest argument he ever had to rebut. Then Jack's attorney wound it up, pointing out the inconsistencies and irregularities. After hearing both sides, the judge called a recess.

Jack's attorney told him, "This could go bad for you. Do you want to accept a lesser fine and go to jail for a year?"

"No, I want to see it through."

Jack knew I was there and he trusted me. The judge, instead of imposing a $500 fine and a three-year sentence, fined him just $50 with no jail time. Then they forgot to assess him the $50.

The song I learned in the river has to do with the fangs of a snake. A snake comes at you with what looks like two tongues. The Creek translation for the song means, "It's going to turn to fire and consume your words." That's part of that chant and that's why the prosecutor ran out of words when he started summing up—the song paralyzed his thought process.

Before I would ever use this chant to help someone, I'd have to determine the rightness and fairness of the situation, so I serve as sort of an attorney, too. In this instance, I felt really clear in my mind that Jack didn't need to be punished because the sheriff had come up behind him without identifying himself and telling him he was under arrest. Jack defended himself instinctively without knowing who was grabbing him. If it seems justice isn't being served, I can come through on occasion. That's part of using the medicine ways responsibly.

REAL SNOW

I was asked to bless a ski resort in Copper Mountain, Colorado, a few years ago because there hadn't been enough snow in eight years to make the resort profitable. It was operating but going downhill, so they asked me to come up there and bless their land. As I was driving through New Mexico on my way to Colorado, there were snow clouds in the sky above me and I spoke to them, saying, "I want to meet your relatives at Copper Mountain. I'm on my way there." On the evening of my arrival, it began to snow. The next morning I did a ceremony and it really started snowing heavily. I would not allow any cameras or audio taping during the ceremony, but afterward, the news media came. Even the TV stations reported it, and a reporter from "A Current Affair" interviewed me and showed what was accomplished after I performed that blessing ceremony.

The resort owners who had asked me to pray for snow are my friends—they give me a place to stay when I'm in that area, so I was happy to help them out. If I was that kind of a person, I could have capitalized on the many phone calls that came from all over the nation after the TV show aired, but I always need to be clear about my motivation for helping people. The resort staff screened the calls for me, but there was one lady who got through and asked me to pray for her to receive abundant riches. She said that if I did so, she would set me up for life. If she'd just said, "I need to meet my obligations, I have many," maybe we could have worked something out. But if I accepted her offer to "set me up for life," I would be taking advantage of the medicine ways to help myself, and that goes against our teachings.

I did not direct what the Great Spirit should do with the weather at Copper Mountain; I just made an appeal. I don't predict and I don't take credit for what the Creator does. The snow that fell showed that a communication can still be made to the Creator, but people miss that—they look for great magic, or tricks, or whatever it is that they have in mind to call it. One interviewer asked me if it was magic and I told him, "No, it was just snow."

In medieval times, it was said that, through alchemy, base material could be changed into gold. St. Germaine was the greatest alchemist who ever lived, and he stressed the fact that when we appropriate these powers for mankind's use, then we are responsible to the Great Being for how we use them. Likewise, my elders taught the same thing—we must not misuse these powers because we have to answer for everything that we do.

The basis of all alchemic action is the transference of energy. If you freeze water, it becomes ice, but it's still water. There's a transformation that takes place from one form to the other. Similarly, you can appropriate the power of clouds and everything they contain to produce rain, sleet, or snow. That's what I was asking for and that's what happened. If you take care of the sacred trust that your elders passed on to you in the beginning, then you can make an appeal to a Higher Power and get results. But along with that there is a great responsibility.

We may seek power to dispense certain knowledge that can help people. We can call in the wind, rain, snow, or fair weather. Maybe we'll need the rain to let up for a while so we can get through with some other part of a ceremony. Such things involve power, but whose power is it? *To become powerful is to allow a Greater Power to work through you. But seeking power just to be considered powerful—we don't even talk about it.*

WORKING WITH ENERGY

The medicine ways are multifaceted. There are many, many energies that we deal with and some of them may seem even more mysterious than changing the outcome of a court case or bringing on snow.

There's a place known as Willcox Playa in Arizona where people have reported seeing mirages such as buildings, trucks speeding upside down, and people dancing. One person even saw a Southern Pacific train running across the Playa, then disappearing into the earth one car at a time. The train he saw was part of a mirage because those things have actually happened in the past.

A mirage is a reflection of something that has existed in another place and time in the physical world. If it's not a reflection of something that existed in some other time or place, then it's a hallucination. People have seen the Empire State Building way out in the desert—that's a mirage. Such events are considered mysteries, but the answer may be more logical than we think. The atmosphere, the Earth's surface, the refraction of light on a curve—all this takes up the particle composition of the atoms and places them elsewhere. The vibratory consistency of the various atoms in all things never goes away. I think it's possible that some day there will be a machine that will tune in on voices that were uttered years ago, like the voice of Moses and the voice of Christ, because that vibration, that energy, once it is created, just stays.

What Western society calls "inanimate objects"—rocks, jewelry, clothing, even furniture and buildings—my people regard as living entities because there's energy within them that's alive. We call stones "rock people." I had an uncle who could put rocks in his hand, sing a song, and when that song was over the rocks would jump around in his hand. These "inanimate objects" can hold energy whether it's visible externally or not. These days, many spiritual people are fond of collecting rocks and crystals. *When you receive something solid from the earth like a rock, a crystal, or even jewelry, you don't always know its history or what kind of energy it has accumulated, so it is best to bury it in the earth for four days and on the fifth day dig it up—by then the energy in it will be cleansed.* Afterward hold it in your hand and put your own energies into it for something good and then it's yours. It's the energy that you put into it that really counts. *If you want to clear the energy of an item made of fabric, let it sit out in the sun for four days.* That will take care of it.

I knew a man who committed suicide and, shortly after his death, I was with his people, helping them pray. They did a traditional giveaway, distributing his clothes and possessions to his family and friends. I told the people there to cleanse those objects for four days—to put the solid objects in the earth and fabric in the sun. That way, the negative energy that caused him to take his own life would be cleared and wouldn't affect them.

But some old, sacred objects aren't meant to be cleansed or ever found again. A couple from Albuquerque brought some artifacts back from an archeological dig in Mexico and a short time later they heard rattling in the room where they were kept. The wife called me up asking what to do and I had them bring those artifacts to me. I cleaned them up and told the couple, "First chance you get, you take them back." Energies were put into those objects to keep them from being misused. In fact, at the time they were forced to leave their homelands, my tribe buried many of their medicine objects with songs of protection so that only qualified people, knowing our medicine ways, could get in there and dig them out. That's how they were put away. So there are a lot of things to think about when you go digging for artifacts.

THE DARK SIDE OF POWER

We regard our sacred areas and ceremonies very highly, but it's said that, in these good places, the powers or energies on the dark side are always lurking, trying to get in. These are energies and people who don't like the light side of things, they don't want people praying, especially for one another. Some practice these dark powers to bring about disastrous results in the life of those people they think of as "too good."

People who are in the work of helping others often seem to be targets for those who don't practice our way of helping, but from all my years of training, I have a sort of built-in protection. If anyone gets really, really mad at me, as long as I don't retort with the same kind of energy, something bad happens to them. I don't do it, they do it to themselves. If I'm taking care of the medicine in a good way, that is the Great Spirit's way of taking care of His own.

When my tribe speaks of witchcraft, that term includes shamanism, sorcery, magic, and wizardry. We refer to people who practice these arts as witches. Many people believe witches are evil, practicing the black arts, but what makes witchcraft good or bad is up to the individual using it. There are white witches with a positive identity, so the story I am about to relate is not intended to place anyone in a particular category.

One of my adopted sons invited me to speak to the student body at a major university. After my lecture, I was told by one of the school officials that a group of people wanted an audience with me and that, since it was not a part of our contract, it would be all right if I refused. When I said that I didn't mind speaking with them, he added, "I have to tell you these people happen to be witches."

"That's all right with me."

He said, "Remember, you're on your own now." As if this was something new to me!

"Okay. Well and good."

Thirteen of them came in—thirteen comprises one cell including a high priestess and a spokesperson. Their spokesperson said they had listened to my lecture and had detected a strong spirit within me and wanted my permission to use that spirit.

"Well, if there's enough to go around, you're welcome to it. There's only one thing—mine happens to be positive, so if you try to use it in negative ways, it will backfire and won't work."

As I was saying that, one apparently wanted to try out his

power and put me to the test. I felt a wind about two fingers wide come toward me, and just before it hit my lips, I blew it away. I knew what was happening—he was trying to choke me. When I blew it away, it went back on him and he immediately began choking, couldn't catch his breath, and had to walk out to the hallway. I followed him out into the hallway, where he was still gagging and choking on the floor. I blew my eagle bone whistle at him and he stopped choking, then I fanned him with my eagle feather and he started breathing normally again.

My training has prepared me to cope with all kinds of situations. What most people call an aura I refer to as my shield and, in this situation, it served as my protector. Since my spirit is positive and for good only, I could not be vengeful. Whatever that young man tried to do to me merely backfired on him.

I brought him back in and said, "You evidently didn't believe me when I said your actions would backfire. I knew immediately when you tried to choke me. There are just four words I could speak and they would be burying you tomorrow, but if I did that I would be no better than what you tried to do. I challenge all thirteen of you to zap in on me at one time. Together you're bound to have a certain amount of power. The reason negatives seem to work all the time is that there are no positives to stand up to them." They didn't accept my offer.

I had to study some of the witchcraft ways of my tribe in order to be able to help people who are victimized by it. I had an uncle who married into the Euchee tribe and got involved in a dispute over some land. Someone got so mad at him that he hired a sorcerer to exact revenge. The sorcerer instructed the man to dig up my uncle's footprint from the ground where he had been standing, take the footprint out into the forest, and find a tree that had been struck by lightning. The sorcerer got wood from that tree, built a fire, and sang a chant with my uncle's name on it, then he put that footprint in the fire. In a few days, the bottom of my uncle's foot began to get hotter and hotter. When he put it in water, the water would get warm. When he put it in ice water, in no time the ice would melt.

My uncle went to the Indian hospital in Claremore, Oklahoma, but the doctors there were baffled, so they sent him to a dermatologist in Tulsa. That doctor couldn't do anything either, so my uncle came back home and contacted me. He said, "Nephew, I want you to help me." I went to see him and by that time the problem had spread up his leg to his knee. The tissue was dying and dropping off and had formed a smelly puss that wouldn't heal. He couldn't walk or even stand on his feet anymore.

I told him, "I want to be truthful. You know I try to help people, but I must also realize my own limits as far as what has been entrusted to me to do. What I'm trying to say is this—if the person they hired to do this to you is still living, I can help you. If he has died, I can only help you so you can live with it, but I can't cure you. If you want to find somebody else who can, why, it's all right with me."

"No, no. I want you to treat me."

I had to use my own powers of visualization to figure out what had happened to him, because he knew he had been witched, but he didn't know how. Then I had to locate the poison that had settled inside his body by saying a chant over and over as I looked for the poison. In this case it was a smelly mass that moved around inside him, leaving behind little pimples and boils on different parts of the leg. After locating the poison, I made two incisions and sucked out the poison.

It took intensive treatment for two months before he got to feeling better. I sang cooling songs into a bucket filled with water and herbs so he could apply it to his leg to make his foot feel better. I also fixed tobacco poultices for him. It took about three months to renew some of the tissue that had rotted and sloughed off his leg. In four months' time he still had scars, but he was walking again. It wasn't my power that helped him but, as an instrument, I was able to use powers entrusted into my care.

In our medicine ways, we can't use these powers for ourselves alone, or else the medicine will not work to help other people. We must never regard this medicine as ours—we are merely channels through which the Great Power helps other people achieve a state of well-being in mind, body, and soul. When we use medicine, we're subject to the One who has control of all power.

When power is misused to hurt others, our people say you always pay for it in one way or another. If you use it out of envy or out of revenge, you can cripple someone, and when you do that, you pay for it, maybe in the loss of a loved one, or some great tragedy to yourself or to your bloodline. And if nothing like that seems to happen, at one point, when you leave this Earth, you're going to have to face the One who gave you this power in the first place, and He's going to ask, "I gave you certain knowledge, certain power. How well did you use it?" You're going to have to answer Him. You can't lie.

6

DOCTORING

How does healing take place?

Jesus took some of his disciples to another country where they found people healing the sick and one of his disciples asked, "How can they do this? They are not one of us." Jesus answered, "Those who are not against us are for us"—meaning that if we have a like faith in a central belief system, then we are not against one another. And it is not the people who were doing the healing—the God they called upon was doing the healing. Native people of every continent go through their rituals—shaking gourds, chanting, drumming, dancing—trying to connect with the One who can heal. There are many factors involved, but the belief of the patient also must be there because that's what initiates the healing process.

A man who was born blind was brought to Jesus. The first thing Jesus did was spit on some dirt and put it on those eyes. Then he told the blind man to go and wash in the pool of Siloam. When he did, his eyes opened and he could see again.

Where was the healing? Was it in the dirt? In the spit? In the pool? If it was, why don't we make a pilgrimage to that pool now? Or use dirt and spit for blind people?

Jesus, being the Son of God, had divine powers. He could have commanded those eyes to see again; he didn't have to go through all those steps, but he did. The placebo effect was taking place. Every step increased the faith of that blind man: "This is going to help me. This will do it." Eighty or even 90 percent of that healing came from within the patient. It wasn't the dirt, or the spit, or the pool. That patient had within himself the necessary power to open the way to make healing a reality.

Suppose you had a throbbing headache and I said, "Hold this stick for two minutes and your headache will go away." You come from a culture that has to prove everything—this must square with that—so you analyze it as you hold it. "What in the world can cure me of my headache? The color here? The kind of wood? The length of the stick?" You're still analyzing it and two minutes later you still have that throbbing headache. But let's say you respond with, "You told me that if I hold this, my headache will go away. I'll do that." Finally two minutes pass and, sure enough, your headache is gone. What healed you? Was it the stick? The color? The kind of wood? You had it within you to cure yourself in the first place and I just pressed a little button for you to make yourself well.

Whether it's a physician or a medicine person, a doctor's own energy has a great deal to do with the healing process. You have to believe that the medicine is going to work out the way you're fixing it. There must be no doubt whatsoever. Regarding the chants and the knowledge of herbs that are entrusted into our care, the elders told us that when we're treating a patient, "Never let doubt come into your mind. This medicine was handed down from generations before us and it first came from the Source of all life, so if you doubt, you're doubting His power. Don't project your own weaknesses, because you're not drawing it from yourself, you're drawing it from a Higher Being who has all the power necessary to heal. Don't ever think, 'It *might* help.' Think, 'It will.' This has helped many people; it's going to help this person."

If you have a negative feeling inside, the patient can pick up on that negativity—I don't care how wide the smile is on your face. When you're attending someone who's sick, it's very important, whether you're a medicine person or not, to be a positive force and initiate positive feelings in that other person. Your positive energy must go along with your own belief that "this will work the way I'm fixing it." Attitude is part of the medicine, so you must have faith because all medicine comes from the same Source.

A GIFT OF TOBACCO

We were taught that if someone wants to apply for our services in the medicine way, whether it be doctoring or teaching, let them offer tobacco—just one small pouch is all that's needed. I once went to Agoura Hills in California to do a house protection ceremony for a woman who had been having a lot of bad luck around her home. A mutual friend suggested she contact me, and he had told her it's proper to give the medicine man tobacco, so as soon as I walked in the door, she handed me a grocery sack from Safeway full of Bull Durham tobacco. She never gave me a donation beyond that, and I didn't bother to explain that the tobacco isn't payment for services, it's an integral part of the ceremony.

It doesn't look like much when you give a pouch of tobacco to a medicine person, but it does a lot of things. First, it serves as a permission to appeal to the medicine ways. Even if the medicine way I perform takes only a few minutes, how long did it take me to be able to do that in a few

minutes? And what sacrifices were made on my part in order
to learn it and earn the right to use it?

So, the tobacco first is permission, but it's also my protection, because I'm dealing with a Great Power in healing
work. If I'm treating a serious illness, it's up to me to ground
it, because if I don't, it's possible that it might get into my
system. And if it is not grounded, the wind—even though the
wind is my mother—might take it to someone in my bloodline. So that tobacco is protection for me and my family.

Another thing that happens when a medicine person is
presented with tobacco and asked for help is that his knowledge and training are activated—he shifts from being just an
ordinary human being to an instrument through which the
Great Power flows. "Which one of these approaches and
techniques should I use in order to enable me to help this
person?" That tobacco allows me to come up with something
that will work—it provides a way for me to connect with
the patient and know what he needs. If the medicine I fix
calls for tobacco, I will use the same tobacco the patient gave
me. Otherwise, I don't need to do anything else with that
tobacco after it has done its work of establishing the connection between us.

And then, after that, in the tradition of my tribe, a donation of some kind is made. We never used to call this payment, we called it "exchange for medicine ways." The term
in our language is *helis a gaga*, "goes with medicine." Medicine by itself may not work unless the patient or his family
gives something in exchange for the medicine and what it
took for the medicine person to acquire that knowledge.

My teachers told me that if someone gives you something
in exchange, all right. If not, these medicine ways are alive,
and whether the person puts tobacco in your hand or not,

you try your best. Maybe some just don't have it, but they might bless you later on. *You see, in the way of my people, it's hard for us to say thank you with nothing in our hands. We always want to give something in appreciation.* In my case, I rely on donations because I don't charge money. My own people know the different types of medicines and what should be given in exchange and they give accordingly. Back before money was given, sometimes they would give a hog, several chickens, or some piece goods along with a ham. If the illness was such that the medicine man had to spend several days or even a week or more with that person, he would give as much as a team of horses. That was considered a fair exchange—it wasn't thought of as payment because medicine people never set fees; our people just knew what was an appropriate donation. Still, my teacher had already told me that this would happen, that not everyone would make an exchange and it is not our way to ask.

By not giving something in exchange, a patient clearly disregards what it took for the medicine person to attain the knowledge that helped him. If I didn't know much, it would take me longer to explain it, but if I know right away, it doesn't take long to explain it. I see this happen lots of times—"He just spent a little time"—because this society is time oriented and people get paid by the hour. They don't know what sacrifices the medicine person had to go through, what a long time it took to get that knowledge in the first place. If they had to go to a health professional, it would probably be $75 on up for one visit. Thirty minutes' time, you pay the full price anyway. Maybe they got more help from a medicine person than a health professional would have given them, but when it comes time to donate something, there's a big hang-up.

I don't take it as an affront personally, but sometimes I feel very sad about how people treat the One who really does heal and give. Is that all they think about Him? How do they live their own lives? They have a lot of possessions, but who's behind them? Everything we have—materially and spiritually—comes from the Creator. People often seem to forget that. Those thoughts go through my mind many times. Then it goes out after I've thought it. "So, put all this behind you. The medicine takes care of it down the road someplace. Go ahead and do your best." That's what my teachers told me.

Native Americans have used tobacco as an instrument of prayer for a long time. When they first saw tobacco, they viewed it as a very sacred, unique plant and they knew that the Creator had some special purpose for it. They dried it, then prayed with it by holding a piece of it in their hands and communicating with the Great Spirit, then they let the tobacco float gently to the ground.

The method used today to dry tobacco has never been improved upon since Native people first dried it; it's just done on a larger scale. Eventually we created a holder using oak leaves; we put bits of tobacco inside and rolled it like a cigarette. Later on the Sacred Pipe was given to us and we began using the Pipe in communication. We didn't smoke anything like "pot" in the Pipe—it was just pure tobacco.

That's why this tobacco is very important in our lives. When things are not exactly as we want them to be, sometimes we say, "This is my situation, I need your help," and put the tobacco down on the ground, placing things in His care.

Once I needed a center tail feather from an eagle for a particular ceremony. I was passing through Albuquerque at the time and I went out to the zoo, to the aviary, and I held tobacco in my hand as I spoke to the eagle there, saying, "I have great need for just one of your feathers. Somehow through your relatives flying above please make it possible that I might receive one feather. I will honor you and all living things with it because I want to use it in a good way." Then I put that tobacco down and I went on. Several days later I returned home and found a package waiting for me. It was from a friend of mine, an Oklahoma artist I had once helped.

When I helped him, he had given me what money he had in his pocket at the time—he wasn't really prepared and I didn't ask. But in our Indian way he knew to give something of value, so that wasn't all he wanted to give me. I unwrapped the package and inside was a center tail eagle feather, so I immediately went outside, put down tobacco, and said, "Thank you." *Whenever we pray for something and receive it, one thing that our people are taught to do is say thank you. When you do that, many more blessings come.* If you ask and you get, but then don't do anything about it, He doesn't really appreciate it. It makes it harder to get other things. But the more we show our appreciation, the more blessings we get.

People wonder why tobacco, which is sacred to Native Americans, plays such havoc with the health of non-Indians who smoke. For one thing, when my people pray by smoking tobacco, we don't inhale. Also, one of our basic teachings is "Control thyself." Moderation is a valuable attribute. Learn to develop self-discipline so you don't go hog-wild with any one thing. You can overeat, oversleep, overwork, and overplay. Instead of recreation, which is based on the concept of "re-creation," it becomes more like *wreck*-reation. So we live by the credo "All things in moderation." Water is good for you; we can't live without it. But try drinking a bucketful at one time and see what happens. You have to use some wisdom.

There're All Kinds of Ways

Our people learned their healing ways by going up in the mountains to fast and sometimes having visions and hearing instructions, which they brought back. That's how we first learned about herbs and how to allow healing to take place. When the missionaries came to this continent, they said, "That's all superstition. We present this Bible to you. You take this Bible instead of all that superstition."

So we took the Bible and read it and said, "Oh boy, what a bunch of superstition in here."

"What do you mean?"

"Here's manna falling from heaven, there's a burning bush that would not be consumed, and here's the Red Sea parting."

"Oh, no, no, no, that's not superstition."

"What is it?"

"God has the power to communicate in any method He chooses."

Well, wasn't God communicating with us as He spoke to us through an animal or a bird? And if it is only superstition, then why has the United States Pharmaceutical Department accepted 637 of our herbs for use in modern medicine today? They don't really have an answer for that.

I have an eagle feather that I use in ceremonies. I can look at that feather and know who needs help in that ceremony without having to look around. I can put cedar down on the coals and use my feather to fan the smoke toward that person and help the situation without having to touch him.

Long before the Chinese introduced acupuncture to the Japanese, they had a method called cupping. They would take a cuplike vessel, put flammable liquid in it, light it, and then run it over the patient's body to get negatives out. We aren't that smart. Our medicine people use live coals—we put them in our mouths and blow on the patient. Or sometimes we remove poison from a person just by locating the area and sucking the poison out.

It's said that my great-grandfather on my mother's side had a deer horn fixed so that he could put it on the trouble spots and the horn itself would pull things out. He was in charge of that kind of power.

My people have always considered touch to be therapeutic. If a certain part of the body is in pain, we place one hand in front of the patient's body and one hand behind him, then let the front hand push in as the back hand pulls out, then, reversing the hands, moving them back and forth like an accordion. That motion generates electrodes within the body—the patient can feel energy build up and there is a cleansing of the area that alleviates pain. Four years ago the chief surgeon at Johns Hopkins found out that when you do that, blood rushes in and alleviates pain. He told the nurses to do it and they're practicing it now, but my people have been practicing it for a long, long time.

A lot of our medicine ways have disappeared. We had a real good medicine for diabetes, but the land where I used to get it has been sold and bulldozed over to build a shopping mall and I don't know of any other place where it grows. My mother was a midwife who brought many children into the world and she had many songs, which I never learned—to me they were women's ways and I don't know if anyone else knows them. She used one chant in particular to fix a kind of belt that a woman, after having borne a child, wore around her waist to bring the stomach back to its natural shape. If a child had a stomachache, my mother would sing a little chant and thump the child's belly four times and the ache would go away. You see, a lot of things we can't even explain. We can't explain why an earache stops when there's no medicine; there's just a chant and a blowing on the ear. What's happening?

I have an adopted Cherokee brother who's a psychiatrist in Oklahoma City. We have a mutual friend we wanted to take to lunch, but when we went by to get her, she was going to forgo that lunch because she had a terrific earache. I said, "Let me fix it." I said a chant and blew in her ear and immediately she was all right. "Oh, I feel better now. I can go."

All during lunch my psychiatrist brother was trying to analyze what canal and what anvil inside the ear were affected and how the healing could have happened. Even though he was a Cherokee with an Indian heritage, he grew up with the values of the "modern society"—everything has to be investigated in laboratories, written down, and answered logically. Fortunately, my people don't worry about trying to find out how things work. We don't overload our elders or teachers with "Why this?" and "Why that?" We never question, we just accept.

When I'm working with a patient, I first must diagnose the source of the problem because I'm going to try to treat the cause, not just the effect. Where does it come from? And maybe I just look without even speaking because I'm contacting the subconscious while the consciousness is somehow diverted. In that way I know just about where the problem is. How I am going to approach it is another thing—some situations require treatment beyond chants and herbs.

When I was living in Oklahoma City, I knew a doctor whose wife went into a coma after being in an automobile accident. She'd been in the coma for over a week when he asked me to come see her. Being a doctor, he had everything squared away with the hospital so that I could go in there with my paraphernalia. At her bedside, I prayed to the Creator, then I touched her forehead with my eagle feather, right in the pineal area, which many people refer to as the "third eye." Each time I touched her forehead, I brought in energy from the Four Directions—East, South, West, and North. Then I fanned her with my eagle feather and told her husband, "I'm going to blow my eagle bone whistle four times. Right now another consciousness has taken over. Her own consciousness is still around but she's not using it— it's taken off and I'm going to call it back into her body. When I'm finished, I want her to wake up and be aware of things."

Standing at her bedside, I blew the eagle bone whistle four times—to the East, South, West, and North. To reinforce it, I drove a few miles east, got out of my car, and blew the whistle again. Then I drove back to the hospital and did the same thing—driving a few miles in each direction and blowing that whistle. The next day she came out of that coma and had regained 80 percent of her memory. Twenty percent she doesn't really remember, but at least she was able to function again.

While she was in the coma her consciousness was still

around, but she wasn't using it. It's analogous to getting hit hard on the arm and having it go numb. The arm is still there, the veins and muscles are still working, but it's numb. Proper circulation needs to be revived in that area so it can function once more. What I did was come in contact with that consciousness and call it back into her body so she could become aware again.

THE LONELY ROAD

Helping so many people can take a lot out of you. You're treating this one over here, then you get back and someone else needs help. Dave Lewis told me long ago, "I'm sending you on a very lonely road. No one really will ever truly understand you. They think they know you, but they don't know what you're thinking about, they don't know the feelings that you have, how sometimes even in a busy, crowded place you need to make certain contact, and to do so, you need to be somewhat withdrawn. That's why, in a social situation it's very uncomfortable for you just to sit down and talk to pass the time: 'Oh, yes, this and all that. Oh, isn't it wonderful, and, my, I saw a beautiful chair in the store window the other day. And, gosh, the way they were dressed.' These aren't things you can relate to when you carry medicine. So it's sort of a lonely road, but in the end, it's worthwhile. It's all worthwhile."

One time I had been up two nights in a row in all-night ceremonies helping some people out. Then I drove home, a little over two hundred miles. Talk about tired, I was dead tired, and went straight to sleep. About ten o'clock that night I was awakened and told, "Someone wants to see you." When I walked into the front room, a twelve-year-old boy was waiting to see me. He had asked someone to bring him to my house and he was crying. "Could you help my grandfather? He's really sick, we think he's going to die. I love my grandfather, I don't want him to die. Could you please help him?" Tired as I was, I couldn't say no.

I went with him forty miles from where I lived and it took two nights to attend to his grandfather. Finally his fever broke and I fixed some soup with chants to increase his appetite so he could gain strength. A lot of things were taken care of in those two nights.

The life of a medicine person is full of such things, and if I had a chance to do them a little differently, I don't think I could. Everything is worthwhile. For those services, the boy didn't know about presenting tobacco, but he presented his heart to me, which was all right. He said, "I don't have much, but I have this feather. I want you to have it." That's the eagle feather I use today when I bless people, when I bless houses, when I bless different events. I always carry that feather with me because it's a gift, not only from a child, but from Above. It made its way into my hands, and it's a powerful feather; you can feel its energy even before you touch it. That's how things happen in the life of a medicine person. The sparkle in that boy's eyes was thank you enough for me. I was glad that I was still around to help someone like that.

I once attended a ceremony for an old lady who was very ill. I looked down and saw a lot of troubled things coming out of her. More than any physical thing, she was sick with heartache, so I just put my hand on her head and I prayed in my own language. That was all I did. A month later, I happened to be in that same area and that lady was up and walking around. I guess she had been out to the sheep pen and on the way back saw me. She didn't speak much English, but she hugged me and said, "Wait here." She ran in and came back with a silver hat band and gave it to me. It wasn't the hat band itself that touched me, but the eyes that were saying, "Thank you."

I go to ceremonies where I sometimes hear people pray for me: "We want him to live a long time, be with us a long time because we need him." That's the strange part, like I'm supposed to live just because I fill certain needs. I'm not taking it wrong, I appreciate the prayers, but I remember one occasion when my Cheyenne nephew in New Mexico prayed for me: "I want my uncle to live long and enjoy himself in life." He was praying for me not only to live a long time so I could be of help to people, but to live to the time when I could really enjoy myself. It meant something to me to hear such a prayer, that I could enjoy myself as a human being.

And as a medicine person I will always do that because I have a commitment; I have a sense of dedication to my work. But the prayer that I might enjoy life has a great meaning to me because medicine people get tired like everyone else; we have our ups and downs. When I was ten I worked hard all day long on my two-acre cotton patch. I was full of energy then—I could go for hours and hours, and when I went to sleep, it was a beautiful sleep because I had done something constructive, and in the morning I was ready to go again. *When you have a good purpose and reach for that purpose, it makes life worthwhile to live.*

7

ANOTHER KIND OF HEALING

THERE IS A GOOD STORY FROM THE NAVAJO PEOPLE OF years ago. Today it seems that every Navajo has a pickup to drive around the reservation, but in earlier times they used to get around in wagons pulled by small horses, known as Indian ponies. They'd ride for miles to get water and haul it to their hogan and more miles to the trading post and back.

One old Navajo rode a long distance to go to the trading post. Since the post didn't have much exposure to traffic, the owner really liked to talk when he got a customer. They were talking as the Navajo brought his groceries to the counter and they talked as the trading post man was sacking the groceries. As the Navajo paid him, the man was still sacking and talking, sacking and talking. The Navajo finally made the long trip home, and as he unpacked the groceries, he discovered that the money he'd given to the trading post man was there in one of the sacks.

Early the next morning when the trading post man was about to open up, he found this Navajo waiting for him. The Navajo handed him the money, and the man asked, "Where was it?"

"It was in my sack."

"Thank you, Chief. I sure appreciate this. I want you to

know I really and truly appreciate it. But I'm curious. Why did you bring it back to me?"

The Navajo pointed to his chest. "In here. I got two little men in here. One's good, but the other one's sure bad. He's a bad little man. The bad one said, 'Keep it.' The good one said, 'It's not right.' The bad one said, 'He won't miss it.' The good one said, 'It doesn't belong to you.' They argued all night last night. Tonight I want to get some sleep."

We don't label such things as "conscience," but our elders taught us that there are different personalities within us that manifest at various times. Humor can be a powerful way of teaching also—we're going to remember something that we laugh about, and I guess that's why many of our teachings had some humor in them. Sometimes our elders would paint word pictures to make things ridiculous when they taught, and even when they counseled with people.

Just a few years ago I tried that with a lady who claimed to be suicidal. She called me up one winter day in New Mexico and said, "I'm contemplating suicide." I knew her well enough to get by with this: I told her, "As long as you're contemplating suicide, go ahead and contemplate, but don't commit it because look outside. There's a blizzard going on. The ground's frozen. Talk about digging a grave! You wouldn't want us to go out there and have to dig a grave for you in this cold weather, would you?" I just kept going on and on about how ridiculous it would be to die at that particular time. She started chuckling and said, "Oh, heck, what's the use," and slammed the phone down. But she didn't commit suicide and is living a good life today.

There are all kinds of ways to handle life situations. Sometimes people need encouragement and sometimes they need shock treatments; there are times when people need to laugh and times they need to cry and you have to know which is called for when you're counseling someone. To make people laugh, they say that's medicine, too, and now in modern psychiatry they're trying to do the same thing. When you make people laugh, they've forgotten their troubles momentarily and it's kind of like a shot in the arm.

The healing arts are not only a matter of learning to use the chants and herbs, they also entail learning how to pinpoint certain areas that a person is dealing with emotionally—something that's really troubling their mind. To learn about life, to learn about people, you never get through. You're always learning. You think you know all about certain subjects and then something may be pointed out to you by a child that makes you aware of what you've been overlooking. What really qualifies a person to study the medicine ways and to heal not only physically, but to counsel with people? How do you counsel with people?

When I was still living in Oklahoma, I knew a man who was leaving to do missionary work with the Navajos. His station wagon was all packed and his family was in there, ready to take off, when he asked me, "What can you tell me about the Navajos? I know you go out there a lot. What can you tell me about them that will be useful to me?"

"You ready to leave now?"

"Yeah, I'm leaving in about three, four minutes."

"You want me to tell you what will be helpful to you in your missionary work in three minutes' time?"

"Yeah, can you?"

"Yes, I can tell you. First of all, capitalize on that which you have in common with the Navajo people."

"I may have something in common with the Navajos?"

"Yes."

"What?"

"Well, you are a human being, and the last time I checked, they're human beings, too. You have that in common. You're going to be preaching to them thirty or forty minutes, maybe an hour—I don't know how long-winded you are—and in that length of time the old people in the Navajo tribe are going to be watching you and they're going to know all about you. They're going to take you apart and put you back together again. They'll know more about you than you will know about them. So if you promise them something, you be sure to fulfill that promise. Treat them as fellow human beings, not as a great preacher looking down on these poor souls, but on the same level as a human being. That's all I can tell you."

On another occasion, a man came to me and said, "Say, I've been called to preach."

"Wonderful, who called you?"

"God."

"Why, that's even more wonderful if He called you. So when are you going to start preaching?"

"That's what I wanted to see you about. I need some seminary training, at least two years. But my daughter's graduating this year, and next year my son graduates. Meanwhile, I'm working at a service station barely making ends meet."

I said, "Wait, wait. Before you go any further, I know exactly what you can do."

"What?"

"Go back and tell the One who called you about all these problems. Maybe He didn't know about them when He called you, so you tell Him."

You may ask, "What kind of counseling is that?" If he's genuinely called by God to be a preacher, there will be a way provided. But if he's having doubts now, what is he going to do in the name of the ministry if he goes wrong later on? I didn't tell him all that. I don't always go into detail and explain a lot of things. I merely pinpoint something they ought to think about.

God Is Forgiveness

I took graduate classes in psychology for three and a half years. I needed just another half-year to get a degree, but I only took the courses I wanted to take and then I left. I did that mostly to compare Western psychology with my teachers' approach so that, should my practice extend beyond our own people to non-Indians, I would be able to speak in a language that they would understand.

I'm an adjunct consultant at the Psychiatric Memorial Hospital in Albuquerque, and in certain situations at the hospital, I work with the patients. One was a nun who left the convent because she fell in love—she wanted to get married and lead a family life rather than following the ways of the order. When she left the convent, the priest told her, "You will never be forgiven. You will go straight to hell." That seed was planted there and it germinated until she got to the point where she thought she was possessed by the devil. I had to work with her intensely to redirect her line of thinking to believe in the greatness of God's power, of how God must be thought of not just as a God of love, but also as a God of forgiveness, and that He has the power to dispel the dark forces that seemingly enter us.

I told her the story of Jesus being confronted by a man who lived among the tombs, shrieking all day and night and cutting himself with stones. They tried to chain him, but he would break the chains and people hated to go near him. Jesus went over to him and cast the demons out of him. I told her, "That power has never lessened. It's still in force if you're willing to believe. *Love and forgiveness are synonymous. There's hardly any division at all. God likes to forgive— when we say 'God is love,' we can also say 'God is forgiveness.'* It means the same thing. You can't truly forgive unless you really love. You can't truly love unless you can truly forgive. That's how the matter stands."

She finally understood, and I told her, "The priest is only a human being. He's meant to interpret God's love, but as human beings we can all make mistakes. It's not my place to say he made a mistake, but he misinterpreted something to cause you to think this way. The devil is very, very powerful. He seems even more powerful when we're too weak to stand up to him, but we have something at our command that can stand up to him, and that is God himself, the Creator. He can stand up to darkness if you will allow Him to. Out of your love for life and the love of your life you wish to make a home with, you want to be all right, so ask God's help to take care of this situation for you." Then we prayed and I "cedared her off" by fanning her with my eagle feather and cedar smoke. After a while she got her thinking turned around and now she's happily married and has two children.

According to professional ethics, a minister doesn't go into the field of the attorney and a doctor doesn't go into the field of the spiritual—that's the minister's realm. But in my case I can go in any direction. That's why I'm kind of a handy thing to have around a hospital.

LOOKING AT THE WHOLE

There are two types of thinking—spatial and linear. Neither one is any better than the other—it's just how you happen to think. In linear thinking you take one item, then keep adding other items to it until they build up to a whole. But in spatial thinking you take the whole and then see how it became whole by filling in individual units.

I was once giving a workshop at a center that had a very good cook and on the last day we had a ceremony during which one of our group publicly praised this man for his cooking. I would call that linear—singling out one member of a family. Immediately I said, "Yes, I agree. We did enjoy the food very much, but the inspiration to cook with love comes from your home, from your wife and children, who support you. Even though they may not be with you in this kitchen, they're cooking with you because of the love that you share in your home." That's spatial—acknowledging the whole family, not just one member of the family.

Our elders always seemed to look at the complete whole, whether they were treating someone for physical illness or emotional problems. They looked at the overall picture, then determined what was out of balance within that whole and they were more or less able to pinpoint where the trouble spots were. It wasn't only the medicine people who understood this, but any elder could evaluate so he or she might be able to help another person. They can be very blunt, saying, "Did this ever happen to you?" Or, if the person seems real sensitive, then they would begin telling them, "I knew of a person who had a situation where this happened to them early in life and this is how it affected them." It's a way of communicating among my people that ensures a person will get the message without getting defensive and resenting what you have to say.

As an example, suppose I'm sitting in a circle with a group of people and among them is my nephew Robert, and he has done something that I didn't approve of. Let's say he had started drinking heavily. Also in this circle is another nephew, Walter, who hasn't done anything bad to my knowledge, but for Robert's benefit, I'm going to say to Walter, "Nephew, I'm going to tell you about a few things. Should there ever come a time when you're feeling sort of down and you're looking to liquor to give you some comfort, I want you to think twice about it. I knew a man who had a lot of stress in his job because his boss was really hard on him. As a result, he started drinking every night as soon as he got home. Next thing, he took a drink in the morning to fortify himself before he went to work. Then at lunch also. After a while the company fired his boss, and he would have been next in line to take his place, but because of his drinking, they fired him, too. Since he couldn't support his family anymore, his wife took the children and moved in with her parents. Now he's all alone and in a real sorry state. So if you ever find yourself in that position, think about these things I've told you, about what can come from trying to drink away your troubles."

Those who have been around our tribe long enough would know that "he's telling someone off in here." But they wouldn't say anything because, in our tribe, we don't talk back to our elders, we don't argue with them or question their judgment. We just sit there and take it all in.

Meanwhile Robert begins to fidget. "I'm doing that very thing. Gosh, I'll know better next time." That's a form of teaching in our way—saying it indirectly. Because if I address him directly, Robert may not say anything to me verbally, but he'll be getting mad, and when he gets mad, that's a distraction from what I'm trying to implant in his mind. So I shift it over somewhere else so he can take everything in and retain it. That's one way we counsel.

RELEASING AND RELINQUISHING

Many things happen early in life that affect our behavior, attitude, and thinking, and our elders were aware of all these things. If a person's life seemed haphazard, seeming to have no true direction, they'd ask, "What's wrong with this person? Didn't he have any training at all, any kind of a teaching?" Or they might ask, "Early in life, what kind of a relationship was there between father and mother and child? Was there a domineering father or a father who was tolerant and understanding? Was he interested in what the child did in school, or did he say 'yeah' and go on to other things? Did the child have a nurturing mother who was always a haven from the cares of his little world? Or was the mother intolerant, overbearing, abrupt?" They go from there, putting in the various units, and if one doesn't seem to fit, then they know that maybe this person has had an experience early in life that still bothers him and needs to be taken care of.

There are many things that happen to us in our early life that stay with us. A little child is all alone in a room full of toys. His parents look in every once in a while to make sure the child's not getting into trouble, then they go back to their soap or whatever they're watching, too busy to really be with the child. But if the child knocks over a lamp and breaks it, the parents come in yelling and screaming. That's the first direct interaction they have with the child. Such lack of interaction is what's known as abandonment—the child is ignored until something negative happens, reinforcing the idea that to get any attention or love the child has to be bad. The parents never say, "That's good, you're being good, playing good." As the child grows, he has it bored into him that he's bad. He wasn't born that way, he's learning it: "Perhaps I really am bad." That's the beginning of the low self-esteem we often hear about, but many fail to see how it begins. There are all forms of abuse of children—sexual, physical, psychological—but the most basic, the most common, is abandonment.

Or maybe early in life you really wanted something so very dearly you'd just do almost anything to get it. Maybe you thought that if you were really extra, extra good, you might be able to get it. If you were really, really good and didn't get it, you were just good for nothing and that disappointment stayed with you. Years later, when you experience something similar to this event, you go to pieces. You don't know why you react the way you do, but it's something that happened a long time ago that makes you feel so bad. You're still holding on to it, much like a monkey holds on to a banana.

A witch doctor from South Africa told me how they catch monkeys there. They bore a hole in a pumpkin large enough to slip in a banana, then they reach through the hole with a spoon, clean out the inside, and drop in the banana. When a monkey comes around, he smells the banana inside the pumpkin, sticks his little forearm in there, feels around, grabs hold of that banana, and then he's stuck. His brain will not tell him that to free his hand he's got to release that banana. He just holds on.

That's the way of a lot of human beings today—holding on to that banana for years. You haven't let go of your old hurts and disappointments. There are many, many things that happened in your life that you should have gotten rid of, but you're still holding on to them, you still have a big dialogue going on. No wonder you have wild dreams at night. It looks like a kaleidoscope going through your mind because you hold on to so many things that you should have let go of a long time ago.

Now what happens? You are given a choice when you hold on to that banana. A choice either to let go or to blame that stupid old pumpkin: "If it wasn't for that pumpkin, I'd be out there free."

Blame started when Adam was created along with his helpmate Eve. You know the story. The Creator used to walk with them in the cool of the evening, but one evening they weren't around, so He started calling, "Adam, where art thou?" Adam wasn't about to say, "I'm right here." He was hiding. God already knew what had happened, but He was putting them on the spot, they had to answer for their actions. "What happened here?" Adam began to blame God: "This woman You gave me." This woman *You* gave me. *You're* to blame. I guess they did something that was natural to do, but apparently it wasn't the right time for it.

So the blaming started right there; we humans inherited that. We like to blame situations and people for our problems. But if I'm blaming other people, what am I doing? The word *blame* really means "giving responsibility for." If I'm going to blame you for my misfortunes, I'm turning all of my emotions over to you and saying, "Here, you take care of them." But are you qualified to handle my emotions? They're my emotions, why don't I handle them? It's easier to blame someone else. It's not too easy to look at yourself honestly, and that's why most of us still hold on to that banana for years and years. Let go once in a while.

My people say never point a finger of scorn or judgment at your fellow man because when you point, there're three fingers pointing back at you. You might be three times worse than the one you're pointing at, so look at yourself first. That was our teaching. My people don't point anyway, we hate to point. The elders say if you point, your finger will grow crooked.

There are many, many ways to let go of our bananas, so to speak. *The way my people take care of something that we're not happy with is to honor it and say, "Thank you, you've taught me a lesson."* If it's anger, if it's hate, if it's a drinking problem: "Boy, you've been with me for a long time. Now I'm going to try something else. But I want to thank you for teaching me something about myself." Never try to just get rid of it. You can't, it's too strong, it's too embedded. Instead, honor it and say, "Thank you."

My tribe had a Drunk Man's Dance to convey the message that "We respect you as a great power but we'd like for our people to do other constructive things. To honor your power in having taken hold over our people, we're going to create a dance just for you." We also have a ceremony for warriors returning from battle or, in modern times, the armed forces, where they were exposed to much death and bloodshed. We say it weighs heavily on the mind when someone witnesses death, so this ceremony washes away the negative feelings and sense of loss. If you fill that space with something else, what you're doing is employing the law of physics that says no two things can occupy the same space at the same time. So get it out and put something else in. *If you've got a negative, put a positive in. They can't both be in the same place at the same time. Clean it all out.*

Many of our hurts and ills come from our thinking structures, our attitudes. We've been hurt once, so we don't trust anybody because of it. Trust takes a lot of effort. But once you get to that point of trusting, then if the people you trust don't live up to their end, that's their problem, not yours. You trusted them, and if they let you down, then accept it and go on to others. If you stay at that point of betrayal and hurt, you're not going to grow. Move on to other vistas, other opportunities.

I knew a man who was mad because he had loaned some money to someone he thought was a friend and it was long past the time when the friend should have paid it back. I said, "Whoa, wait a minute, wait a minute. Before you point a finger at him, let's consider this. You had the option to say no when he first asked you. So let's start there. You allowed this to happen. You created the circumstance. Say to yourself, 'Yes, I did it.' I don't know how much money it was. If it was a lot, it was a costly lesson. But it was a lesson nevertheless."

We learn from these experiences. *Be grateful for all the difficult situations in life because you can learn something from each one.* When you learn and say, "I did it," and you accept that fact, then you have dealt with something that's been nagging you for years and years and years. You have finally let go of the banana of that situation and it doesn't come and nag you all the time.

A lot of self-help books and seminars tell you about your problems and your unresolved anxieties. "You need to release these things." Release, release, release. But they seldom talk about relinquishing, and that's just as important as releasing.

Let's say I have something I cherish very highly, an heirloom that's been handed down from generation to generation, and I'm the last member of the family to have it. Now suppose I have a friend who's been down in the dumps—her lip is so low she could step on it. I want to lift her spirits, so I say, "I'd like to make you happy. This has been in our family a long time and I want you to have it." So I give it to her, hoping she's happy with it. I've released it from my possession into her possession.

Okay, well and good. Some time later, I go shopping downtown and pass by a pawn shop and right in that window there's my family heirloom. "Darn! That's been in our family a long time. I gave it to her and now it's over here. I'm feeling real hurt." Why? Because I released it, but I didn't relinquish it, I still have sentimental attachments to it. On the other hand, if I thought that this person needed help but was too proud to ask for it, and I felt good about making it possible for her to get help, it means that I've released *and* relinquished.

When you release and relinquish, then you're okay. But if you just release, it will keep coming back, over and over and over to bug you. Relinquish if you really want to release.

HE KNOWS THE STREET YOU LIVE ON

Back in Muskogee, Oklahoma, I often visited the Veterans Administration Hospital to talk to the shut-ins and I was practicing my medicine ways in a different situation. Here were veterans who wore the uniform of our country and exposed their lives to danger so that we can enjoy this thing called freedom—freedom to move around, freedom to make a living, and if it be our choice, freedom to be into drugs or alcohol. It's freedom nevertheless. Those veterans insured that we had that freedom when they gave the oath to defend our country, even if it meant death. Then they came back, bodies all torn and wracked, and they were just lying there. On special days when families got together, even Memorial Day, they didn't get as much as a card. These were the people I used to go talk to:

"I just came by to let you know, comrade, because I was in the service, too, that we don't forget about you. And it does not matter if you feel as if no one thinks about you. The One who carried you through all of these experiences and allows you to live today, He knows about you. He cares for you.

"There was a man named Saul who was a very educated man, spoke several languages, and knew the law. He had an obsession against the Christian people. Much like Custer had an obsession against the Indians, and Geronimo had an obsession against the whites, here was this Saul. He was on his way to a place called Damascus because the people congregating there were Christians.

"While he was on his way, a great light blinded him and he fell to earth and had an experience of conversion. Saul went on to Damascus a blind man, and God sent a man named Ananias to go attend to this man Saul, who later became Paul, the great missionary. When God spoke to Ananias, He said, 'Go to the street called Straight and inquire in the House of Judah for a man of Tarsus named Saul.' Just a little verse like that tells us that our Creator knows the very street on which we live, the very house in which we live, and the various needs with which we live. He is there to supply that help for us. He knows the very hospital, the very ward, the room, the bed that you abide in. He remembers, He knows, and that's what counts."

This patient couldn't speak—he had been shot in the throat—but he spoke to me nevertheless, loud and clear, with his eyes. When he reached out and squeezed my hand, he said a great deal to me. That communication from a heart to a heart, a soul to a soul, is worth more than a whole page, a whole volume of books that could be written.

In our Native American way, medicine is not just a bunch of herbs or the training a physician receives. It's helping people attain that which is good in life. If you can point them in a new direction, saying this is the path, this is the way to go, that's a form of healing. *When you give a lifting hand and make someone feel better for it, you've given that person medicine.*

8

WALKING IN BALANCE

THIS IS A SOCIETY WHERE WE LIKE TO GET DEPENDENT ON professionals. If something goes wrong with you, you go to the doctor. I'm not trying to take any food out of the doctors' mouths, but there is much that you can do on your own. As much as you can think yourself sick, you can turn it around and think yourself well. We haven't explored even one-eighth of the mind's potential. We'd rather pay out good money so we can be told by a professional, "This is what's wrong with you." We feel good about it, except for the money we pay.

Still, you haven't really been cured—internal problems cannot usually be handled by external means. The cure was already within you, but we've never been taught that we can handle most of our own problems.

People often ask for my advice and counseling, but overall, the best advice I can give to anyone at any time is: Never complete a negative statement. You might start out thinking it, but don't complete it because you're about to enter it into the computer up in your head and it could come true.

Your "subconscious" responds to whatever you put into your conscious awareness. When you put information into a computer, it responds to that information and you see it on the screen. Similarly, there's a crew of workers within

you—sub-personalities, or whatever you want to call them—
who are going to see to it that whatever you put into your
conscious awareness comes out that way. So if you put in
something negative, it's going to come out negative. When
a captain on a boat gives a command, the crew below
doesn't argue with the captain, "No, I think you ought to
go this way or that way or at this speed." They don't say it's
right, wrong, moral, or immoral; they just respond to what
they're told. What you feed your subconscious can transfer
not only into your attitude and your thinking, but your
body, in time, will feel the brunt of it. Particularly if it's
heavy-duty stuff.

We attract. The situation that you are most afraid of you
are going to attract. Some fear is healthy because it makes you
cautious. But when you're overly afraid of something, you're
going to attract that very thing.

When people come to me with various problems, I have
to determine if that problem is psychosomatic or if there is
some part of the physical body that is in need of help. There
was a clinical psychologist who worked in the Indian hospital in Shawnee, Oklahoma, who had made one of the tribes-
men angry at him. I don't know what he did, I didn't ask,
but the tribesman told him, "We have ways of dealing with
people like you. I'm going to get you." A few days later the
psychologist's leg drew up and he couldn't straighten it out.
He was sent to St. Anthony's Hospital in Oklahoma City and
was placed in the psychiatric ward because the physicians
could find no physical cause for the problem.

My nephew was the head of the Tri-State U.S. Indian
Health Service in Oklahoma City at the time, so he called
me and said, "We have a doctor in here, a psychologist from
Shawnee. Would you help him?" I went over to see the psy-

chologist and he told me about what this Indian said he could do to him. I knew that the Indian had just threatened the psychologist and never actually did anything, because when I examined him there was nothing planted inside his leg. The doctor actually did it to himself unconsciously.

I told him, "As a psychologist, you know good and well what took place. He planted a seed in your mind—'We can do things to you'—and that seed germinated into a reality. You know about transference, when the mental changes into the physical, and this is the case here. Whether you own up to it or not, you were scared and as a result your leg drew up. I'm going to undo it with four songs, then I'm going to blow my eagle bone whistle four times in four directions, and then I'll fan you off with this eagle feather. After the first song you'll start moving your leg. With the second song, you'll be able to begin to stretch it out. And by the time I finish the fourth song your leg will be straight. Then I'm going to give thanks with this whistle to the Great Being who really helped."

And so that's what happened. I started singing, and even before that first song was over, he was already moving his leg. By the third song it was straight. With the fourth song, all the tingling had finally left and he felt all right. Then I fanned him off with my eagle feather. Afterwards I told him, "Don't tell the doctors what I did. Let them try to figure out what they did right."

When you plant a seed, it attracts everything necessary for its germination. It gets nutrients and moisture from the soil. The hard coating of the seed becomes soft and eventually falls off. The shoots go deeper into the ground and in time a stem grows upward until it emerges through the topsoil and begins to absorb sunlight. The seed has attracted all it needs for its growth. Planting an idea in your conscious awareness is like planting a seed. The subconscious responds by attracting all the things necessary to bring that idea, whether positive or negative, into fulfillment.

I did some counseling at a place in Houston for AIDS patients called the Omega Center. The very first thing I did was tell them to change that name to something else. Omega is the last letter of the Greek alphabet. It implies that this is the end—change it to something else.

THE POWER OF THOUGHT

We still have a lot to learn about the mind. I'm not talking about the brain—I'm talking about the mind. There was a soldier who lost his leg during the Korean War. His leg was amputated at a mobile surgical unit and they had to bury it because of the fighting going on around them. After he was back at the base hospital he kept complaining that ants were crawling all over his leg. The doctors told him about false pain and all that, but he persisted: "Ants are crawling on my leg." To placate him, a detachment unit was sent to dig up the leg, and when they did, ants were crawling all over it. The leg was several miles away, the body here. Where is the mind-body connection severed? These are things we don't know yet, but just as the body can communicate to the mind, so can the mind affect the body.

People often wonder why they have so many aches and pains or so many difficult circumstances surrounding them. We create them, but by the very same token we can take care of them with our minds.

Thoughts affect the body and some of the senses within the body. For instance, suppose you get hungry, make a sandwich, and take it outside so you can take in the sun on a windy day. You forget to bring something to drink, so you leave the sandwich on your chair and dash back into the house, get your drink, and hurry back out. You're so hungry that as you sit down you bite into the sandwich and begin to chew. In the time that you were gone, sand has blown on the sandwich and you find yourself grinding the sand between your teeth. You see? Just thinking about it gives you a shivery reaction in your body. Thinking affects the body, so it's important how you think and what you think about.

Suppose you had a falling-out with someone you perceive as obnoxious in every way. This person sees nothing good in anybody. Finally that nothing good was directed at you and you took offense. You find it very hard to forgive that person and thinking about him brings up your stored anger. Now imagine another person who did something really nice for you, not to get something out of you, but just to make you feel good. A great deal of respect was shown by that action, and you love that person dearly. So here is my example: you experience anger when you think of this obnoxious person and then you turn right around and feel love when you think of someone else. You did not change your emotions, you just changed your thoughts and your emotions followed. So thinking does affect our emotions as well as our bodies. That's why *it's best to know what you're putting into your conscious awareness because all of it is energy, vibrations.*

There are many, many levels of vibrations in and around us. You can go out to nature, away from the busy workaday world, where you think the night is really calm and still but there's a lot of activity taking place on different levels. The night may be still, but it doesn't mean everything has stopped. In the same way, your mind never stops. You can only slow it down sometimes.

A Good Night's Sleep

If you have had a very exciting day, when you go to bed your body is tired and you may go right to sleep, but your mind picks up more speed. If you studied rapid eye movement, you know there would be a lot of activity in your eyes. Why do you wake up tired some mornings, and other mornings you feel rested even though you slept the same amount of time? You wake up tired because your mind was accelerated all night long, dealing with all kinds of dreams flashing back and forth, trying to tell you something. In the morning you make yourself get up, but you drag around all day. Even at work, where you know your job inside out, you just can't hit it with full force.

So how do you take care of these inner issues? As you are about to go to sleep, relax your body. It does not matter whether you begin at the top of your head and work down to the bottom of your feet, or start from the bottom of your feet and go all the way up to the top of your head. Just relax every muscle along the way, and as you do that, take deep, slow breaths. Breathe in soothing, calming thoughts, like a soft wind blowing in, caressing and lulling you into a deep, restful sleep. Then imagine as you breathe out that you are releasing all the tensions and stress from your daily tasks. Release them out into the atmosphere and put all the unfinished business on hold for the time being. It will still be around tomorrow—you can tackle it then. But for now, put everything on hold and take care of your body; allow it a good rest. This way you relax not only your body, but also the thoughts and feelings that go on within you.

And as you lie there, be grateful for the day you've had and ask for a good peaceful rest. Put that into your conscious awareness, and when you drift off you'll go into a deep sleep and you'll feel energized the next morning. You might even see your problems from a different viewpoint. What you thought you couldn't see the end of will become a little light at the end of the tunnel and you can go on from there. You really can handle these things for yourself.

We have tapped very little of our mind's power, a very small portion. Not because we have such a little mind, but because we don't rely upon and utilize it enough. *The mind has the power to do anything. It's better than any wonder drug that's been developed for any reason today.*

LAUGHTER IS THE BEST MEDICINE

One of the most notable attributes of my tribe is their sense of humor. They're a great people who always find something to laugh about in spite of difficulties in their own lives. We're taught early in life to laugh *at* ourselves and *with* others. We don't poke fun at other people, we poke fun at situations where we can all laugh together.

At our funeral meetings, before the service, you'll often see some group laughing because someone has said something funny. But when it comes time to be serious, they're there in all sincerity, respect, and honor for the deceased and the mourners. They find a balance between tears and laughter. When someone tells me a sad story, I'm really touched, I go along with it for a while, and then I change to something that is a little lighter. I try to keep myself in balance all the time.

There are people who don't know how to laugh; they're doing serious work all the time and then they don't know why they feel so run down. It's because they've been operating on just one level; there's no balance. You never see them smile. They worry five days ahead. They worry about today, tomorrow, and the next day; that's how far in debt they are to their own worrying process. It's one thing to be concerned and find ways to do something about a problem, but worrying is like sitting in a rocking chair. It gives you something to do—you can rock, rock, rock—but it doesn't get you anywhere.

Some people read heavy books, one after another. It's really an imbalance. I read plain old westerns, then I'm ready to read something like Carl Jung's God's Answer to Job *and I can just drink it all in.* Then I leave that awhile and I'll get back to a lighter topic. I sometimes read the comics because they often tell a story truthfully and directly. I sometimes draw my own cartoon of something I'm thinking about, then I throw it away. It's served its purpose, it's relieved my mind, and then I can go on to more serious things.

In the most somber situation you can almost expect something to turn around—if we don't balance it out on our own, a situation often arises which forces us to.

I knew a Ponca woman whose husband passed away. In the Ponca way the deceased is buried on the fourth day, but up until then people stay up all night and talk. They take a short break at midnight for refreshments, then they convene again and go until morning. It happened that one of the preachers from a nearby church got through talking just before midnight and was on his way to sit down. Being elderly, he was taking his time. It was the widow's turn to speak and as she was thanking the people for coming, the preacher finally sat down, leaned back in his chair on the slick floor, and kept going backwards until he fell under the casket. The other speakers got up and pulled him out. The widow kept a straight face until she couldn't hold it any longer and she just burst out laughing and everyone laughed with her. She said, "You know my husband who's lying here would really appreciate that. He was that kind of a fellow, jovial—he liked to make people laugh." That was the great thing; she turned it around into something good.

Two Parts to a Whole

There are usually two parts to a complete whole—day and night are parts of the complete whole called time. Guilt and nonguilt are both parts of the complete whole we call judgment. Just go on down the line—there are two sides to most every situation in life. Try to balance them out.

Eastern philosophy talks about all people having yin energies as well as yang energies. Whether you're a man or a woman, we each have some of the opposite energy within us. Water is thought of as yin, but when frozen it becomes yang and yet it started out as water. The transformation is subtle, no great dramatic thing, yet it's there. Most medicine people don't often talk about this, but a medicine woman needs male energy and a medicine man needs female energy around them, especially when they're making medicine. It makes that medicine strong.

Among the Navajo, when a man attends an event or council where an opinion must be formed, he is accompanied by his wife or eldest daughter. They say that because men and women see things differently, a balanced opinion can only be formed by a man and woman together. When a Navajo medicine man performs a blessing ceremony, there's a certain part of the ceremony when a woman related to him must repeat the prayers right after him. Female and male energy connect to make that prayer strong. This applies to almost all medicine people. We don't often bring these things out and talk about them, but they're there.

Working with opposites can also bring your physical body back into balance. Sometimes you come home from school or work feeling tense and stressed out. The easiest way to relax yourself is to put the left hand at the base of your spine and the right hand in the curve where your head and neck meet—just hold them there and you'll begin to feel relaxed. Placing your hands that way connects the positive and negative poles of the nervous system, and the energy flowing back and forth balances the body and calms you down. If you sit awhile like that sometimes, you find you can almost put yourself to sleep. That's a simple way to help yourself relax—you can even do it at work. But don't reverse your hands—if you put the left up top and the right at the bottom, it works the opposite way, it makes you irritable.

You can be most effective if you're balanced. People who write me often end up with a New Age saying, "Walk in balance." But do they know how to walk in balance? If your brain's too focused on one side, you may be walking around at an angle yourself. By opening both sides of the brain, then you can walk in balance.

You may have heard about the left and right hemispheres of the brain. The left side is logical and there's nothing wrong with logic. The right side has a connection with the ethereal, the spiritual aspects of life, and the two sides of the brain must be kept in balance for you to lead a balanced life. All through school from kindergarten on up through your

Ph.D., you were taught to function from the left side—you had to be writing all the time, making reports. Writing your thesis, you had to refer to someone with a degree who had already written about it so that you could quote them to let people know that you're well read and did quite a bit of research. You used logic all the way through school because the teachers wouldn't quite accept "The Spirit told me to answer it this way." If you went to the ethereal side of your nature they'd throw you out of class because you weren't quite right in their opinion. So we never got a chance to use this spiritual side very much.

My people didn't talk about left and right sides of the brain—we didn't even say brain, we just said there're little people inside of us. There's one side that's always figuring things out and has to have answers. The other side has more faith, trust, and belief.

Native people learned to connect with their ethereal side early in our history. We learned, not through scientific laboratory experimentation, but through what we sensed around us, through being encouraged to trust our instincts. Sensing things was our salvation—we relied on those senses. A warrior might sense something behind him, look around, and sure enough something was there. Everyone still has these senses—they're not as finely tuned as they were in the past, but they can be. Relying on your senses can be your salvation in your business, your life, and your work. The first thing you feel like doing comes from your instinct, your right brain. But then a flood of logic comes in from the left brain. If you let your logic ruin your first instinct, you may pay the consequences.

Suppose you are going out and you start to take your jacket. It's right by the door and you're reaching for it with one hand as you open the door with the other. When you open that door, the day is sunny and clear, so you tell yourself, "I won't need this jacket," and you leave without it. Then during the day the weather changes and it gets cold. When you left, your instinct, your inner senses, told you, "Take your jacket." But your logical side, seeing the sunshine, said, "I won't need it." So it's often better to go along with those first instincts and try not to analyze too much. *If you practice using your instincts with small things, such as whether you need your jacket, you will eventually be able to rely on them for the big decisions in life.*

I mentioned earlier how our elders would take young people to a tree in the woods blindfolded, then bring them back, take off the blindfold, and ask them to find their tree. On other occasions, before taking a group of boys out to the forest, our elders would tell them, "This is our meeting place. Before you venture out, love this place, put your heart into it." Then they'd blindfold them. But this time when they reached the woods, the blindfold was not taken off. "Find your way back to that meeting place." They would have a stick to use in front of them because they were like blind people. The only way they could find their way back was by experiencing the love they felt before they went out.

As you arrive somewhere, see if it feels right in your heart. If it doesn't, then change direction. Keep following what feels good to your heart until you find that place again—you know that you've arrived at the right place when you feel that love that you had before you left.

Life has many directions. It's up to each person to choose which direction to go in. The freedom to choose is a great gift. It might lead you to a blind spot, a place where there seems to be no opening, but if you keep trying, a pattern forms and you can always learn to follow your heart. Notice the pattern, notice how your mind works in conjunction with how your heart feels at certain stages in life, and use that as a guideline. Your life may sometimes seem like a maze, but there is a way out. It's about choices. This is truly a case of trial and error, finding a way out of the maze.

LIVING ONE DAY AT A TIME

Once I was giving a group of U.S. Forestry Service employees a tour of our Indian hospital in Oklahoma. This was the higher echelon of the Forestry Service and the group included professors and scientists. One of the professors was looking at an old Indian sitting in the waiting room and said to me, "Will you ask this old man if he's sick?" I didn't know the man, but I knew he was old because when I asked him his age he said he was in his nineties. I asked him in Creek if he was sick. He just smiled and said, "No, I'm not sick. I just look that way."

"Ask him what is his biggest physical problem in his old age."

Again, I asked the question in Creek.

With a smile he replied, "I can't answer that because I don't consider myself old, but when I get old and find out I'll let him know."

Today, people—especially non-Indian groups—are age conscious. They're also time conscious because "time is money." When people ask me, "What time are we starting the workshop?" I always say something like "Eight-seventeen," kind of like Amtrak time. It's humans who try to impose time on situations. When the leaves fall early and seemingly before their time in nature, who's to say that it's before their time? We even try to impose Daylight Savings Time on birds, but it doesn't work. When it's time for them to molt in their season, they molt. When it's time to change color, they do that in their own time, not when we say.

We often hear people say, "I ran out of time." Or, "I don't know where time goes anymore. Here it's already noon and I haven't done all that I was supposed to do." They don't stop to think that we have the same amount of time every day—it's how we use the time that's important. But people don't accept that. They're looking for someone or something to blame when they just didn't manage their time well, they didn't make a plan and follow it. Maybe they made a plan, just haphazardly worked at it, and left a lot of tasks undone and tried to blame it on time. Or perhaps they tried to pack too much in. We all have twenty-four hours each day, whether it's Daylight Savings Time or not, so it's best to look at how we manage the time we have in order to accomplish our tasks. When people have some unpleasant tasks ahead they usually choose the easiest ones first. Why not tackle the hardest ones? Get them out of the way and then you will enjoy the easier ones because you're more confident. When you get the big obstacle out of the way, your day will run smoothly and you can go back home happy.

The reason that I am over seventy-five years old and still going strong is due to the fact that one of the first lessons we were taught was to live one day at a time. We didn't think in terms of years or birthdays. *Live life as though you might die tomorrow. Do what you would like to be doing, and do your best each day.* If you want to be lazy, be good and lazy that day. If you want to be industrious, be really industrious that day.

In our true Indian way, we slept when we got sleepy, we got up when we were ready, and we ate when we got hungry. There were no set times. Today, you've got to get to work early, so you gulp something down real fast and go. That gulping doesn't help you. It might have filled you up physically, but it didn't help you because your mind and your gulping didn't go hand in hand.

Do you ever go to a coffee shop in the morning? Maybe you saw something on the late evening news the night before, but you didn't get all the details, so you're reading the paper as you're gulping down coffee and a bagel. During the day you don't know why you feel so sluggish, but you did it to yourself. Your mind distracted your stomach from digesting the food and sending it to the various body streams to help you throughout the day. It stopped here, stopped there, because your mind was elsewhere.

I was on my way to an executive office in Oklahoma once, and when friends asked me where I was going I said, "I'm going to Ulcer Gulch," because I knew that's what I'd find there. If you're an executive, you go out to lunch with other executive people, talking shop. You talk about whether you should merge with this and whether it would pay to do that and if the stock is ever going to go up because it went down so many points and it had come up a little but not enough to override two days' slump and you're kind of worried about it. You're supposed to be helping this body of yours by eating, so that the food will be transferred into energy that will keep your body going, but much of it has been blocked because you are thinking about serious matters and turning your attention away from your food.

You need to pay attention to your stomach, what you're putting into it and how you're doing it, because your stomach is your biggest help—it's where the energy that sustains your life enters your body. You think you save a lot of time by working while you eat, but then you don't understand why you feel tired and have such bad indigestion. No wonder so many executives have ulcers.

You should also be thinking pleasant thoughts while you're eating, not reading about a war or thinking about the last two days of arguments that you're still trying to resolve in your own mind, or someone who you're at odds with. Maybe you're eating alone, but you have a dialogue going on—"If I ever face that person!" It doesn't matter if you have the most correct food in the world; if your attitude isn't right when you eat it, it's just a waste. You'll have your stomach knotted up and you'll have pains and indigestion because you brought that negative energy into your body along with your food. The old ranchers and farmhands working the fields knew the importance of paying attention to their food—they ate in silence, and after they finished eating the foreman would lay out what was to be done that afternoon.

Our Indian people didn't eat in total silence, but if we spoke, it was on a light note, something funny. There was a man who'd traveled a long way to join his friends for a meal. Instead of asking for the salt to be passed, he reached across the table to get it. Another Indian at the table said, "Pretty far . . . but you made it here." It had a double meaning, and others who knew what was implied started laughing. You can enjoy food like that on a light note.

When our people were forced to live on reservations, fences kept them from their hunting grounds—they no longer had the buffalo, the staple of their diet, so they became dependent upon commodities that were issued by the government. They also had no knowledge of the nutritional value of the processed foods they were given, so they ate what tasted good to them, and maybe overate certain foods. Whatever the reason, our people were plagued with poor health and still are.

Like most Indians, the Pima tribe eats poorly—a lot of greasy stuff like fry bread, which is good from time to time, but not as a regular diet. Yet, in spite of that diet, Pimas never have heart trouble, so scientists studied them for a whole year and could find only one possible reason—they were always laughing and jolly when they ate.

So it's safe to say that it's not necessarily what you put into your body, but the attitude with which you put it into your body that counts. Suppose you go on a diet which is "mind over platter." You're thinking about all the cholesterol and fattening foods you hear so much about: "I can't eat this. I can't eat that." That's negative, negative, negative, all down the line. Turn it around: "I'm going to put into my body what's best for me. I'm going to choose foods that are good for my body." Focus on positive thoughts and your state of wellness can be maintained, not only by what you eat but how you are eating. Prepare your food and eat it with love. That's the way our traditional people did it—whenever they cooked something, they put love into it. They didn't have much to offer, but when people came it didn't take much to satisfy their hunger because there was a lot of love there.

In our culture, whenever we are given food—whether someone buys us groceries or makes us breakfast or takes us out to dinner—we say that it extends our life. And as we accept that food, we breathe a word of prayer so that the dividends of that gift might be multiplied into the life of the person who gave it.

In our way, we are always grateful for food. Whether there is an abundance or just enough to go around, we are still grateful. And we always try to leave the table before we feel completely full. It increases your willpower, for one thing. Also, those organs within you that need to break down the food and carry it throughout your whole system will not have enough room to work if you're stuffed full of food. Overeating puts a lot of extra stress on your organs as they're trying to work, so leave the table just a little bit hungry, without eating everything on your plate. Be good to your body, leave some of your food if you can.

We were also taught to always leave a little food on the plate as an offering—it's our way of saying, "May this food find its way to someone who might be in need, someone we don't even know." We don't make a great dramatic affair out of it. It is not done to say, "Look what I'm doing." We do it because all people live together on the same planet, breathing the same atmosphere—we are all relatives. We leave an offering as an appreciation for what we were able to enjoy, and we want to share it with others who might not have as much. We want this food to find its way to where people of other lands, from the youngest to the oldest, may be provided enough to sustain their lives in good health.

When I was a boy, one of my elders told me, "Notice the leaves on the tree. When it turns cold, the leaves are going to change colors and fall, but they're still part of that tree. When you live long enough, in your maturity, your life is going to be meaningful and others will notice you. Like the colors changing in each leaf, they're going to see you for what you have done in life, and it will be beautiful to see. Eventually you're going to fall, but in falling, you're going to make it possible for other life forms to come after you. When the new year comes, when everything becomes green again, part of that which fell to the ground will be alive. And so it is with life, it goes on and on. What we're actually doing is borrowing the sunlight, the wind, and the food, which comes to us from deep under the ground—the roots reach up and feed us out here on the limb. *So, think of each day as a loan and learn to use it wisely.*"

9

COPING WITH SUFFERING

THERE'S AN OLD STORY ABOUT A FROG WHO FELL INTO A butter churn and, no matter how high he jumped, the top was too high for him to reach. But as he was jumping, his webbed feet created the same up-and-down motion as the paddle, until finally butter was formed and he could stand on it and jump out. Whether it happened or not, it brings out an important point—it's often possible to turn negative situations into positive. Never feel a situation is all negative. There's a counterpart that is positive. Look for it, reach for it, utilize it—it will offset the negative. If you don't think so, go into a dark room and strike one match—it dissipates the darkness immediately. Darkness seems like something that's hard to stand up against, but light is much stronger—just a small light dispels the darkness. That's how it is with everything. If there's negativity all around, find the positive counterpart and utilize it.

There are four great teachings in Buddhism. The very first of those teachings is that life is suffering. We think that it ought to be the other way around, that life should be easy, that it should be happy. That's what we seek, but the stark, dark reality is that life is suffering. And *coping with suffering gives meaning to life—it is what gives us our strength.*

Things may seem bleak at times. We stand outside at night and it's completely dark, we can't see the sun, the moon, or the stars. Then all of a sudden a comet crosses the heavens and lets us know there's sun shining somewhere, because we can only see a comet as it reflects light. In difficult times, we are made more aware of the resources that we have within ourselves and therein lies our peace. Peace is not the absence of conflict. It comes from the ability to cope with that conflict. *And so in the darkest moments of your own life, never lose sight of the fact that the sun is going to shine through to a great day, a great life. Whatever your potential is, you can reach it.*

In the Bible, Jesus once said to his disciples, "Let us go over into Capernaum." So they got in a little boat and soon Jesus went to sleep. On the way a fierce wind came up and the disciples became frightened, so they woke Jesus. The first thing He did was to rebuke them, saying, "Oh, ye of little faith." Then He talked to the winds and the winds calmed down. "What manner of man is He that even the winds obey Him?" Even though they were His disciples and were with Him when He performed great feats, they still never quite understood Him.

Why did He say, "Ye of little faith"? Jesus had a divine connection with the Father, so when He said, "Let us go over into Capernaum," they would arrive in Capernaum because He said they would. But the disciples didn't take Him at his word—they became frightened when they saw signs of danger all around. And that's why "Ye of little faith" meant "You have no faith in what I proclaim, in what I can do. It's still hard for you." Jesus took care of that danger and there is still a Power today that takes care and makes a way for us.

Most of us have very little faith—we say we do until something difficult happens and then we feel everything is hopeless. We try and try, we struggle, yet we feel like giving up sometimes, thinking, "Well, this is it, this is the end, this is as far as I go in life." At times like that, go to the ocean and watch the waves come in. The tide has a steady rhythm, a tempo that's never affected by the storms at sea. When the tide hits the shore it goes as far inland as it can, and when it reaches its zenith it is not the end, it's merely a turning point. It then flows back out to sea, to where there's great strength and power. It doesn't matter how strong the storms might be out there, it does not affect the rhythm of the ocean as it comes in and turns. *In our struggles we may think we can't go any further, not realizing that it is merely a turning point in our life.* All power is available to us. You can turn things around in your own life, live hopefully, and keep that hope going.

Dante wrote a story called *The Inferno* in which a man takes an imaginary journey and comes to the gates of hell, where there's an inscription which reads, "Abandon all hope ye who enter here." If you arrive at such a place, hope is out of your vocabulary. But suppose the judge who sentenced you says, "After two thousand years I'll review your case." There's no guarantee the end result will be any different, and two thousand years is a long time, but that gives you a thin thread of hope to hold on to. That's the power of the word *hope*.

Live hopefully. It does not matter what happens, what your circumstances are, you have something to connect with. When you yourself cannot solve a problem, there's a problem-solver available—lie down on this Mother Earth, she'll caress you. She still gives you energy, and she still says, "Look up to the Creator. Talk to Him, pour your heart out. The answer will come."

Not long ago a woman called me and I went to see her in the hospital. She was a very young mother who had just given birth to a child with no arms. He had webbed feet and scars on his face, and she was wondering, "Why me? Why me?" I had to talk to her for a long time, pray with her, to show her that there was a blessing somewhere in her situation. In our culture, when such children are born we say they are specially blessed. The Creator had a reason for bringing that child into the world and we are helping the Creator when we make the child as comfortable as possible in every way. It's said there is a special blessing when we help someone like that, although that's not our reason for doing it. My people don't even talk about the reasons, we just try to help.

I told her the story of a similar situation where a little boy was born without arms and the doctors asked her husband to stay by his wife's bedside as she came out of sedation so he could tell her. When the time came, he looked at his wife and said, "Mary, we have a beautiful baby boy. But, Mary, he was born without any arms." Mary lay there for a moment with her eyes closed. Then she opened them and, with a beautiful smile on her face, looked up into the eyes of her husband and said, "John, God must have known how much he needed us."

What I'm trying to get at is this—the most important thing is not the circumstances in life, but your reaction to those circumstances. How do you deal with difficulties? Do you resent or do you accept? Honor every situation. There is a reason why things like this happen. But don't be judgmental and put out a lot of blame: "If it wasn't for this and for that." If something bad has happened, how can you salvage it? How can you turn it from negative to positive? When you do that, then you can cope with anything that comes in life.

When something terrible happens to you, say, "Thank you," *because there's a lesson there.* Maybe at the time it was happening you were so mad or upset you didn't consider any lesson. You wanted revenge and payback, or to cover up and justify whatever it was. You missed the lesson altogether. If you got sick and almost died and then recovered, say, "Thank you." Not just because you recovered, but because now when you see someone else who's as sick as you were, you can have compassion that you didn't have before. That was the lesson and you're grateful for it.

I had a friend in Albuquerque who was a radio announcer. He came to see me one day. He was really dejected and told me, "I was fired."

I said, "That's good."

"What?"

"That's good."

"What do you mean? I've been fired from my job, I have a family to support."

I told him, "This is going to make a new man out of you. Take iron ore—there's nothing you can do with it in its raw state. On the outside it doesn't look good at all, so you put it in a foundry where it's heated many, many times until the crust falls off and the core is tempered. The end result is fine steel, and we say that it has been 'fired.' Either we're going to stop with the crust still on or hang in there until it's broken away and we show the world, 'This is the stuff I'm made of.' When you are faced with difficult situations, the crust of ego burns away. Now it's going to show the real you. A lemon has to be squeezed first before it can make lemonade. They either squeeze the best out of you or the worst. It's up to you."

So what does it mean when we're trying to do good and something bad happens? The one we refer to as God is not necessarily testing us, but He allows things to happen to show us what kind of character we are made of.

Not too long ago in Los Angeles, the captain of one of the fire departments was having a prayer meeting in his home. A seventeen-year-old was at the meeting and her mother and nine-year-old brother stopped at the convenience store on the way to pick her up. Two men followed her from the convenience store, and as soon as she parked in the driveway of the captain's house, they came and demanded money and she gave it to them. But that wasn't all. One of the men shot her before he left. The little boy ran into the house and broke in on the prayer meeting. "My mom has been shot." They all ran out, but the mother soon died.

There was a prayer meeting in progress when this happened. If you were praying for something good and this occurred, would you give up? Is it no use to pray? Where else can you go? Where can you get that inner comfort that you're going to need, that inner strength? What fairness is there when someone is loyal and prays to God, yet still tragedy strikes? What people don't always realize is that He goes through our ordeals with us and brings us safely through.

We don't always know how God works. It seems like we walk uphill, find a little relief, and then have to go uphill again. That's one of the songs that we sing to encourage one another: "You've been climbing a hill all your life. It levels and then another hill comes and you climb again. Now I'm praying that things level off and you might see better days ahead."

In His mysterious way a great blessing, something we had not thought of before, may come in and give us the strength, give us the guidance we need. *We should let Him do the driving of our lives—He knows the best way to get from here to there.* Maybe He has to take us by a longer route in order to get there, but it might be the safer way.

In the Bible there is a devout man named Job who believed in the living God. Satan came to God and said, "He's not so much, I can sway him." So God allowed Satan to do whatever he wanted, short of taking Job's life. And all the hardships that you could imagine happened to Job, enough to shake anyone's faith, enough to blame God for the misfortunes and shake a fist at Him, but God did not intervene. Job had great possessions—gone. His ten children died. Maybe other people would have been swayed, but Job's own faith kept him from denying God. And at the very end, after everything was over with, because of his faithfulness to God, he was given twofold of everything he'd lost, and he and his wife had ten more children.

If someone has faith like that, he cannot be swerved from his initial belief. There are times in a person's life when he feels he's come to the end of his rope. Still, there must be a reason for tests, so instead of blaming God and saying, "Have you forgotten me?" accept that the Supreme Being never abandons us. He never forgets us; He's always there day and night looking after us.

Before the coming of Christianity our people felt that they had something spiritually substantial. I'm using the word *spiritual* to mean something that we can hold on to with our faith and not swerve from, regardless of what happens to us. When my tribe was being forced out of what is now Georgia and Alabama on our way to Indian territory, the hardships were severe, and yet our people did not give up. There is one story about a mother and child being left behind because the child was ill and they couldn't keep up with the rest of the group. People hated to leave them, but the soldiers forced the others to go on and the mother and her child were left behind. She kept saying, "Keep up the faith, wherever you go, wherever you are headed, keep the faith going." And out of that, many of our people began to make up songs. "Keep the faith, keep the faith."

Collectively our people were kind of like Job. When everything was lost they didn't lose their faith and their belief in the Supreme Being.

Sometimes our good feelings drain out when difficulties happen, but it is not the end of life. It's a challenge and we go on; we're strengthened. There are many spiritual paths, but only One Spirit. You have the Spirit, don't let go. Sometimes that faith becomes like a little candle instead of a bonfire and the winds come and almost blow it out, but it's still flickering on. And as long as it's still burning, it has the potential of carrying forth the realization of our hopes and dreams. *If we're going to fail, it's better to fail trying than just giving up.*

REDEDICATION

When I was old enough to understand it, my mother told me this story: "When you were a little tiny baby, you got sick and we thought you were going to die. You had a real high fever and I sat in a rocking chair and rocked you all night long. Neighbors wanted to relieve me and take you, but I wouldn't let them, I just held you in my arms all night. Early in the morning, just before the sun was coming up, I took you outside and, facing East, dedicated your life to our Creator. I said, 'If You let this child live, I will do my best to be a good mother. I will raise him knowing something about You and Your great love, so that he can walk this earth and be of help to people. He will be Your feet, Your eyes, Your voice, Your hands. However You can use him, I dedicate him to You now.'" After she came back in the house, the fever broke and I got well.

From that early beginning, a sense of dedication was instilled in me. Many years later, I had to rededicate my life.

I had a son who volunteered for the service. He chose the Coast Guard because it was the kind of service that helped other people in distress. Before leaving for a year's duty in the Philippines, he had a month's leave of absence and came home to visit us. He bought me a new hat and took me to a birthday dinner—we did a lot together in that month.

At the end of the month, on his way to the Philippines, wearing the uniform of our country, his plane stopped to refuel in Hawaii. He sent a doll to his sister, an orchid to his mother, and a postcard to me with hula girls on the front. He knew his dad. He wrote on the card: "This is a beautiful place. I hope you see it someday." He had sent the orchid to his mother because it was May 11, 1964, Mother's Day. He was still thinking of us; he was still thinking of home when they refueled and he went on to the Philippines. Then, during a normal landing in fair weather, due to human error, the plane crashed. Eighty-four men died and my son was one of them.

We got the gifts after the crash, after he had already gone on. Just to touch what he had touched—even the card, how he had scribbled on it—I held it to my heart. There is no way to describe the feeling of loss that engulfs you. And a table that's set with one place missing really takes something out of your heart.

Not too many years afterwards, I went to Hawaii, a fulfillment of my son's wish that I could see it. In Hawaii there's a place called Pele Point, where, according to Hawaiian legends, the winds of the universe have their beginning. Because my mother is of the Wind Clan, I wanted to go up there at midnight, but the guards said, "You can't."

"Why?"

"We close the gates."

I said, "I don't care. I want to go up there."

"We'll take you as far as the chain across the road."

So they drove me as far as they could, then I walked the rest of the way and sang my songs to each of the Four Directions—East, South, West, and North. When I got through, I said, "My mother, when I was very small, dedicated me. At this time I rededicate myself anew to You—from my heart. I will be Your feet, Your hands, Your eyes, Your voice, just as she said. If there's any love that You have, a special love that You want for people, let it flow through me. Let me touch someone and make them a little happier, so that they can be well and walk with good purpose upon this land. Please use me." I dedicated my life again in that way.

When I came back down, the guards asked who was up there with me. I said, "No one." They said they heard lots of voices singing. They heard it, I didn't.

BOOK III

Learning How
to Live

10

THE POWER OF LOVE

DURING WORLD WAR II, WHEN HOUSING WAS HARD TO get and many people had to live in crowded conditions, there was a family staying in a hotel in New York City while they were looking for a permanent place to live. One day their little girl was riding down on the elevator with a man who knew her family and he said to her, "It's too bad you don't have a home." Without blinking an eye, the little girl said, "Oh, we have a home. We just don't have a house to put it in."

A house can be a mansion, shack, tent, or even a dugout. A home is where love abides in the hearts of those who live there.

What is love? What is the manifestation of love? Picture a mother sitting in a room, maybe sewing or reading or watching TV while her little child is playing on the floor with dolls and toys. All of a sudden the child gets an inspiration, runs to her mother, jumps on her lap, and puts her little arms around her. "Mommy, I love you." That is an expression of love from a little child's heart. Can you buy that? Can you force it to happen? How much is that worth in terms of money? It's a little love expressed in the very best way the child knows how, through her own volition: "I love you, Mommy."

Love is synonymous with the word *forgive,* they go hand in hand. Many people quote a prayer from the Scriptures: "Forgive us our debts." But it goes on to say, "As we forgive our debtors." It's a two-way thing.

There's a story in the Bible about the Prodigal Son. His father was a wealthy man, the ruler of the country. The son said to his father, "Everything that's going to come to me, I want it right now, not after you have died." He was the kind who prayed for patience by saying, "God, give me patience and give it to me now!" So his father gave him his inheritance and the son went out in great style with his many friends and then suddenly lost everything. He must have ended up in Atlantic City or Reno or gone into stocks. Buy high, sell low. The money was gone, and so were his friends.

What happened? He got hungry, and when he got hungry, he began to think of home. "In my father's house even the servants have much to eat and more. They can't finish the food, it is so plentiful there, yet here I am the King's son, starving." He got a job feeding some hogs or, as it's written in the Scriptures, swine. They're considered the lowest form of animals in the biblical sense, and he had become a waiter to the hogs. "Here's your food, sir." Have you ever seen a hog eat? They never look up to see where it's coming from because they're enjoying it so much. He almost got down on his hands and knees and started eating with them.

But then he thought, "Wait a minute, wait a minute. I'd just better go home. But if I go home my inheritance is gone and I have nothing coming to me. Now how do I get back? I'll say this to my father." So he rehearsed it in his mind. "Father, I have sinned against you, I have sinned against heaven.

I am no longer worthy to be called your son. If you will take me back as one of your hired servants, maybe I can eat." He didn't intend to go that far, but that's what he meant—he wanted to have some of the good things he had been accustomed to. He got it all fixed up in his mind, not knowing that every day his father was looking down that road, hoping that he would see his son coming back—there was a connection between father and son that never diminished.

On that particular day, as the father was watching the road, there came the son. He couldn't believe his eyes: "Yes, he's coming." He didn't force his son to return, he was coming back on his own. The father didn't even wait until his son came to that great mansion, he ran out and embraced him. "My son was dead, but is alive again. My son has returned." The son started with his little speech: "Father, I have sinned against you, I have sinned against heaven . . . " But that's as far as he got because the father made it easy for him to say, "I'm sorry."

Too often when someone has wronged us, we don't make it easy for them to say, "I'm sorry." "Come crawling back to me and I'll think about it," is often the response. But the father was so glad to have his son back he embraced him and called him "son." They wore sandals in those days, but I doubt the son had sandals by the time he got home—there were too many thorns and stones that he had to walk across to get back. They cleaned him up and put new shoes on his feet so he could walk around the kingdom once more.

Then his father put a robe on him—purple for royalty. He must look like the king's son and carry himself like the king's son. Next he received a ring with a signet that was like a credit card wherever he went in the kingdom. All he had to do was show that signet and he could get anything he wanted.

Then the king said, "Now let us make merry and have a big feast." This story is a great lesson in forgiveness, and that forgiveness could never have come unless there was love.

WHY ALL THIS FIGHTING?

There are two words people use a lot—one is *unity* and the other is *harmony*. You can tie a cat's tail and dog's tail together and drape them over a clothesline—you'll have unity but you won't have harmony. Harmony is a tolerance, a forgiving, a blending—subtle, soft, but very strong. In order to live in harmony, the common denominator that binds is "loving one another" in its truest form.

Look at an anthill with many ants going back and forth. Some ants are carrying things down into the anthill, and after they have unloaded their burdens, they go back for more. There are two lines coming and going, a lot of traffic and many ants. Have you ever seen them bump into one another? Have you ever seen an ant stop to fight another ant, with others jumping in? Even though there's a lot of traffic involved, there's a sense of orderliness, a sense of purpose, a sense of doing something together. They're not just wandering around randomly. Just because they're ants, they don't sit around and expect things to come to them. They're working together for their survival. If our minds are supposed to be superior to the ant's, then why all this fighting?

We talk about war zones and send aid and money to other countries, but the greatest war is in the cities of our own country. We need to study the ant colony and get back to the simple order of life. How is it with us today in our society? Are we too prejudiced? Why is it that if someone belongs to a particular religion or race he can't help someone who doesn't belong to it? What kind of love do they have? It's very conditional love—"Unless you do this I will not help you."

I was in the Rangely Mountains of Maine soon after the area had a big forest fire. The fire was getting very close to a Baptist church, but a Catholic boy got out a hose and saved that church by watering it down. When an earthquake happens, people go beyond racial and belief lines in order to help others. When people help clean up the debris after a flood or a hurricane, they don't stop to say, "What nationality are you? What faith are you?" Everyone pitches in when tragedy strikes. Do we always have to wait for a crisis to be able to truly manifest our love for one another? People talk about unconditional love, but they never talk about nonjudgmental support, which goes hand in hand with unconditional love. Those two go together to express real love.

I used to go to a church where the choir had to march in from both sides to get into the choir loft. Altos and basses came in one way, sopranos and tenors came in the other way, and they had to pass one another until they filled up the loft. There were two ladies in the choir who were not speaking to each other, even in church, so as they passed by, one would look one way and the other would look the other way. And yet the first song was "Oh, How We Love Jesus." If they can't love each other, how can they say they love the One who created them?

If someone is unkind or throws verbal daggers at you, that person has a problem—why make it your problem, too? You might not love what a person is doing, but you must love the person, because if you're going to say you love a Higher Being, you have to remember He created that person also. If you can't forgive, then that's a challenge for you to work on until you can pray for that person and mean it. Then a big load is going to be lifted from you. Until you do that, you carry a nagging, aching feeling all the time. You can't even rest with it at night. You lay and toss and turn and all kinds of dreams come up—your inner consciousness is trying to get through to your brain, but it can't get through because it's all clogged up with anger. It's one thing to talk about love and forgiving, but another to truly forgive. Break apart the word *forgiving*—"for giving." Giving what? Giving love. This is why love and forgiveness are intertwined.

There was another lady who used to sing off-key in that choir. There was a big service coming up, one where there were going to be a lot of guests, and people wished that she'd get sick or go on vacation and miss it. But she was always there, never missed a service. Then one day she died. They did miss her then. Even with her off-key singing, in her own way she was expressing her love. They realized it then and they really missed her. They also found out that she used to get on her knees and pray for each member of the choir before entering the church auditorium. So it's not how beautiful or resonant your voice is—what matters is in your heart, the connection you have. That's what counts.

Many years ago there was a church in Oklahoma City whose deacon wouldn't allow two of our Indians with long hair to come in. I happened to know the pastor of that church and I had a long session with him. I said, "What kind of a hairdo did Paul have? What kind of short hair did Peter have? And what business is it of yours not to allow any person to come in here? I'm not speaking just because they happen to be Indians. Your church has a dress code. Where is it in the Bible that you must follow a dress code in order to worship God?" We had a wonderful talk, and he had a few tears in his eyes when I left.

Some people have a tendency to make more of the rules and rituals than what is in their hearts, which is what really counts. When we pray it's good to have a certain atmosphere—whether it's in a church, praying with a rosary, or in a sweat lodge—but it isn't necessary, we can pray at any time, anywhere. I knew many World War II veterans who became preachers after the war. They said, "We prayed under fire, surrounded by machine guns, mortars, and cannons, with devastation everywhere. Whether you grew up in a church or not, sitting in a foxhole not knowing whether or not you would live to see the next day, you truly connect with your Creator." I heard one veteran preaching a Mother's Day sermon and talking about how mothers are a great part of our lives, no matter how old we are. He said many of his buddies were shot in the foxhole, and as they lay dying, the last word they said was "Mama." The thing that is our strongest connection in life comes out at the end.

So praying is not only following rituals and doing it just right. It's how we feel inside, how our heart connects, and how we live. That's called walking the spirit road. It's not just following a religion, but following the Universal Being of All Creation, of All Wisdom. If we know Him, then we do our best because we have a belief system based on love, and even if we make a mistake we can say "I'm sorry," and He's ready to forgive. When we're afraid of doing something because of the consequences, we're turning religion into fear, not love. The words of Christ were: "I came that you might have life and live it abundantly." To live life abundantly is to feel free.

LOVE HEALS

The power of love—if that love is sincere and true—is the only force that can melt the human heart. Nuclear weapons can destroy people and have long-lasting effects, but love is what repairs and heals. No bomb can do that, it has to come from understanding and tolerance. And it has to come from forgiveness being channeled into the lives of other people, making them feel their worth and stimulating their potential. If you have a lot of love, animals come up to you, even flowers seem to follow you as you walk by, recognizing and responding to love. Love is expandable, it can encompass this whole universe. It can heal.

Many years ago there was a lady of my tribe who became seriously ill and bedridden. In the way of clanship, she was my aunt, and many relatives and friends came around and prayed for her. An M.D. and a medicine man from our tribe treated her, but they were both rather stumped and didn't quite know what was really wrong with her. She slept all the time and didn't seem to have any appetite—she was just wasting away. Some doctors thought it might be tuberculosis, but they couldn't get a correct diagnosis and say, "This is it."

This lady had taken in a young boy who was her nephew, but she was raising him as her own son and he loved her very much. He was not a medicine man—he was not old enough. He was just an ordinary, normal young boy. But one thing that he did have was love for this woman, whom he looked upon as his mother, and he decided to stay with her around the clock. All he had to offer her was running errands, getting her water, and changing the bedding. Other than that he sat at her bedside. On the fourth day of his vigil she awakened from the deep trancelike state that she had been in and her strength started to return.

One of our elders said, "It was the power of his love that caused her healing to take place." Of course, we couldn't take this to a scientific laboratory and prove it—we just took it for granted because there is a great deal of healing in love.

And so we see what love can do. It's good to send out prayerlike energies when we see something that is out of balance in people's lives. If I see some drunk in an alley sleeping it off, and people are passing by snickering and laughing, I can't help but say a prayer: "Take care of him, let no harm come to him. Bless him, so that in time he can salvage the good that You have implanted in him." I don't know the person, his background, tribe, or name. That's not important—what's important is that he's a human being.

I knew another Indian lady who was ill and was brought into an all-night prayer meeting inside a tipi on the Otoe reservation. There were many medicine people working on her all night long. One young man came in late. He was not a particularly religious person—he had gone to such meetings before, but not regularly. He was what we refer to as a "roughneck." But this lady was related to him in some way and, knowing she was ill, he came to the meeting.

Not being used to such ceremonies, he was very awkward at first. There was wood laid out by the fire in the middle of the tipi and he accidentally kicked it and sparks flew everywhere. When he sat down, he didn't sit cross-legged or on his knees to show respect like we do; he just sat with his legs straight out in front of him. As part of that prayer circle in the tipi, the participants usually pray while smoking tobacco rolled in corn shucks—that smoke carries our prayers up to the Creator. It took him a long time to roll his and he spilled his tobacco and had to ask for more, causing quite a distraction. But after a while he got his tobacco rolled up and then he asked to pray out loud for this woman.

"She knows the kind of person I am, yet she's never pointed a finger of scorn at me. She always talks good to me. God, You have need for this kind of person to be in this world. If we had more people like her, maybe those of us who are looked down upon by others would not have reason to feel so bad about ourselves. She's the one who makes me feel good. I don't qualify like these other people who talk to You. But I came here because I love her, and I ask that You look down upon her. You don't have to bless me. But I ask, if it's at all possible, that You bless her. Take away her illness, whatever it might be. You're the One who can do it. That's all I have to say."

The woman had been lying down but soon after that prayer she sat up and wanted to speak. "I appreciate all the efforts everyone has put forth on my behalf. I feel well now, I have no pain, none whatsoever, and what got me well is how my son here prayed for me. What that prayer meant to me most was the fact that there was sincerity and love there. It was like taking good medicine and I'm very grateful."

Love heals, love is what makes things a little better than before. Why do my people feel good about all mankind? Because love is universal. When I use the words *my people,* I am identifying myself with all Native Americans, and especially my tribe. We accept all kinds and races of people, and we love them. Our history is not a beautiful example of mankind's tolerance and understanding toward fellow human beings. My tribe suffered many injustices—being forced to leave the places we called home, enduring many hardships. Yet in spite of all of this, we still hold to the belief that the Great Spirit is a God of universal love.

And once we appropriate that love into our own hearts and minds, then we immediately let it flow through our lives and into the lives of others. We can feel love in our hearts even for the white race because not all white people were responsible for the injustices against our people, there were some who spoke in our favor, just as there are many who support us today.

When our people were about to be removed from Georgia and Alabama, Davy Crockett, a well-known figure in history, walked to the home of Andrew Jackson east of Nashville, Tennessee, and spoke in favor of our tribe staying in our homeland. Of course, we were removed from that area anyway, but his intercession is one example of the white people who were for us. We have come to find out there is always good and bad in every culture, and when we bring this universal love into our own lives we feel better for it.

My great-great-grandmother is buried at Fort Gibson, Oklahoma. She was part of that forced removal known as the Trail of Tears. I don't know which of the graves is hers—there are many crosses there with no names. There is so much anger that I could have in my heart, but I don't. Somewhere along the way I found out about this great love from a great Creator and with that love comes forgiveness.

Why not live a life where you allow that Great Love to come in and work through you? We study human beings, different societies, and how one culture is different from another culture. But now is not the time to look at the differences, but to see how we are alike. Love is the common denominator that goes through all cultures and binds us together. Without it, we're lost.

THE PEOPLE OF GOD

I don't always feel comfortable in talking about Indians; even the word *Indian* itself is very misunderstood. When Columbus found the natives here, they were gentle people who accepted him, so Columbus wrote in his journal, "These are people of God." In his language, he wrote "In Dios." Later the *s* was dropped and Indio eventually became Indian, which originated as "people of God."

So we became Indians because of that, but they often teach in school that when Columbus discovered the new world he mistakenly thought he had landed in India. And even though he hadn't arrived in India, there is a place called the Indus Valley in India and the people there have almost the same language as the Euchee tribe here in North America—many of their words and names for things are the same, even the skin color and texture of a Euchee's hair is like the Indians of India, so there is a connection. I speak twelve Native American languages, yet Cherokee is unlike any Native American language I've ever heard—it sounds more like the Chinese Mandarin dialect, so it makes me wonder if there is some connection between them.

Several years ago I was invited to a conference in Council Grove, Kansas, sponsored by the Menninger Foundation. There were many people there from all over the world, and during the conference a woman came up to me and said, "I'm having a problem. I'm a registered nurse, the profession that I've been trained in and been practicing for several years, but I want to go into another field and I don't know what to do."

I said, "That's your problem."

"What?"

"You think you are throwing your practice and your training out the window, but you are not necessarily going into another field—you are extending your training and practice into a broader field of service." I built a fire and picked up a coal, put it in my mouth, and blew on her hands and dedicated them. "Now it's up to the Higher Being to point the way for you."

Two years later, she created a form of therapeutic touch which is practiced all over the United States today. Her name is Dolores Kreiger, and she has won national awards for her work. While I was working with Dolores, Tulka Tarthung Rimpoche, a Tibetan, was watching me and out of the clear blue sky, asked, "Do you use peyote?" He caught me by surprise; I didn't know he knew anything about peyote. I said, "Yes, I do." He said, "I wondered because in northern Tibet we have some people who use peyote and they use those coals just like you do." I had no idea. It was quite interesting.

The interconnectedness of the people of the world goes way back. Columbus was not the first to come to America. We used to think the Vikings were, but scientists have found some Hebrew writings in North America and they think perhaps the Hebrews were here before the Vikings. It's been said that Native Americans may have been part of the Ten Lost Tribes of Israel. There is evidence of Jews who are Chinese and some in South Africa who are black. Then there are Indian Jews in Mexico and today's anthropologists and archeologists cannot tell you where they came from. That leads me to believe that maybe we *are* a part of the Ten Lost Tribes because of the similarities between the practices of the Hebrews and American Indians. We both fast at our New Year time. When the Hebrews roamed around the desert, they traveled in a caravan with the women, old men, and children in the middle and the warriors outside for protection. That's how our people moved from place to place. They also had skin tents, kind of like our tipis of old. It's possible that the Hebrews were here in North America first and then traveled to Israel, or that we came from Israel to North America.

The number 4 is very significant to Native people—it is a number of completeness. The white, black, yellow, and red races represent all humanity. At one time there might even have been a common race of people who divided and became different colors with different backgrounds. Maybe this was a preparation for each of these races to learn all they could among their own people and then in time we will combine the red, black, yellow, and white into one big culture. And if the Spirit is one, we may not change colors, but instead change our attitudes into the spirit of oneness with all living things on this planet, not only the two-leggeds, but the four-leggeds, the wingeds, those that are in the water, and those that crawl. *It's time to stress the things we have in common with one another, to show how much alike we are. We might be surprised to find that we are truly all brothers and sisters in this universe, and most important, that we have to maintain that relationship in order to survive.*

11

TALKING WITH
THE EARTH

WHEN I WORKED AS A FIELD REPRESENTATIVE FOR A PRI-
vate Indian college in Muskogee, I once accompanied our
glee club to a performance in Chicago. There was a big
turnout and I was to speak during intermission while the
choir was getting their second wind, or whatever they do
during an intermission. While I was waiting in the wings, a
little white boy burst into the backstage area and started
looking in different doors. I said, "Hey, you looking for
someone?"

"Yes, yes." He'd been running and was out of breath. "I'm
looking for the Indians."

"Well, take a good look at me. I'm an Indian."

He took one look at my suit and tie and said, "No, you're
not an Indian. You're human." So I put him on my list—
my prayer list.

LET YOUR EVERY STEP BE AS A PRAYER

As a child I loved to watch the B-class western movies and
my favorite scene was when a wagon train would form a circle because they heard the Indian war whoop. I'd be eating
popcorn, or eating someone else's popcorn, thinking, "Oh
boy, here come those redskins!" They were all around the

wagon train, hollering and shooting arrows, and then the settlers would fire their rifles and three Indians would fall off their horses with one shot—they were very good shots in the movies. Then all of a sudden you'd hear the cavalry trumpet. "Oh boy, help is coming."

Early westerns presented an image of Indians as bloodthirsty pagan savages, and in history we were looked on as wild, animalistic people. In actuality, we never knew we were wild until we started watching those movies and reading about ourselves. We had no concept of "wild animals," because we considered ourselves to be relatives of the four-leggeds. We didn't consider ourselves above or below nature—we considered ourselves a part of nature. Many people don't understand that we had a recognition of the Supreme Being long before the coming of the Europeans and the Bible.

In observing the natural forces around us, we saw that different seasons would come and go at approximately the same time each year and streams ran in certain directions. Today we know that the sun is stationary and the Earth revolves around the sun, but still we say the sun comes up in the east, travels across the sky, and goes down in the west. If there was no Great Power controlling these things, why didn't the sun come up in the north one day and come up in the south the next? There was a pattern, there seemed to be a Power controlling the forces of nature. A human being can blow on a blade of grass and make it sway back and forth, but this Greater Power caused the wind to blow and the great trees to move.

We didn't spend one hour Sunday morning in a religious situation—we spent each day in acknowledgment that every day was a holy day, a sacred day. We have a song we sing in the morning that says, *"I thank You for another day. I ask that You give me the strength to walk worthily this day so that when I lie down at night I will not be ashamed."* It's a song that came to us long before the missionaries.

When our people prayed, it wasn't just for themselves. The blessings would extend to those little children growing up, and for those not even born yet. Our people looked ahead to the future with their prayers, and they considered all life forms as their relatives, even plants, trees, birds, and animals. When we walked on the grass of the plains and fields, we viewed it as being there as a carpet for us, and we respected it. Our people taught their children: "Let your every step be as a prayer."

THANKSGIVING

Before we were relocated to Indian Territory, our tribe consisted of forty-four villages, which we referred to as towns. Today we have fourteen towns still carrying on our tribal ceremonies, and each town has a town chief and a town medicine man, as well as two delegates who represent that town at the main tribal counsel.

There are four ceremonial dances held every year in each of these towns, and when I was a child, my father took me to them. Long before the missionaries came to this continent, my tribe had a ceremony to give thanks for the year's blessings. It was the first dance of the year, our New Year's celebration, held when the earth puts on a new coat of green—new grass, leaves, and flowers. The second dance is for ailing people or soldiers returning from a battle where blood has been shed. The third dance is a time of renewing the arbor of the dance ground—the past year's willow branches that covered the arbor are burned and fresh willows put up to replace the old ones. This is to make way for the fourth and main dance of the year, which is called *Buskitah Thocco*, the Great Fast.

Every year when the corn is just beginning to ripen, the first dance is held to say, "Thank you for another year of allowing corn to grow to sustain our people." We call it the Green Corn Dance, and it is our Thanksgiving celebration— a time of gratitude—and is still held today, with some minor variations. In the old days, we started a fire by rubbing sticks together, and those who were in camp came and took some coals to build their own camp fires so that the people were all connected through the communal coals.

On the fourth day of our encampment, everyone fasted for an evening and a day, then that night we had a dance. The chief of that particular town sat on the west side of the dance area with the town medicine man right behind him. His spokesman, referred to as *heneha*, sat on the chief's left. The *heneha* was very eloquent and probably of the Wind Clan, because they are the orators of our tribe.

When the chief wanted something to be announced, the *heneha* would convey the message of the chief to all the people, and when he was through everyone acknowledged his talk by saying, "Ho." You could hear that word all around the encampment.

In the afternoon of the fourth day of the dance, the *heneha* made an announcement. "We have now come to the time where all of us must be quiet, so please control your children. No loud talking or laughing. This is our quiet hour." The medicine man would then get up and stand there a long time communicating with the Great Spirit, saying that he has tried his best to take care of what has been entrusted to him for the good of the people and that he is grateful that he came upon this knowledge so that people could feel good physically, mentally, and emotionally. We didn't know too much about spirituality.

That was the closest thing we had to a church— it was out there in the wilds where nature was all around. It seemed that even the birds knew to be quiet. Way off in the distance you might hear a bird, but in that immediate area everything was quiet. We were in tune with all of life.

Then the people would dance all night, but when we danced, we weren't just saying, "Hey, let's get up and party." You see, dancing was our way of saying thank you to the Great Spirit—it was a ceremony. The dance area was sprinkled with medicine and was sacred, so before we would dance we would sweat, bathe, and fast so as to be clean inside and out in order to perform before the Great Being.

The ashes from the previous year were scattered all over the ceremonial grounds, somewhat like the story of the great flood as told in the Bible. It was a renewal. Everything's buried, everything's gone—now it's time to make new tracks and give thanks for being blessed another year. All of these elements were brought in, but still our dancing and ceremonies did not set well with the missionaries. They called it pagan, yet it's my belief that however we make contact with the Creator is of meaning in His eyes.

OFFERINGS

All Native American ceremonies reflect our respect for the earth—it is part of our daily way of life. Even today, in our respect for the land, if Native people are going to take something from it, be it herbs, a stone, or earth itself, we always give an offering, usually tobacco, in return. Then we gently take that herb or stone—because this is the face of our Mother Earth that we're marring—and we pray that we will use it in a good manner.

All tribes have their own way of giving thanks to our Mother Earth for the things that she gives to us. Everything we use in life comes from the earth, even the ingredients for the medicine that heals us when we are sick and injured. When we give thanks it's not only to the earth and plant life—we're going beyond that to the Great Power who makes all things possible. That's who we are really addressing and acknowledging—the Creator and all that He has provided for us.

That's how Native people show their respect for the earth. But when the earth and her resources are used without giving any offering in return, then we're faced with natural disasters and the death and damage that follow. I am not saying earthquakes, hurricanes, and floods are caused by human interference and lack of respect. But I do believe that if we pay proper respect to the earth, perhaps when earthquakes do occur, there might not be so much destruction. Maybe the earthquake would happen somewhere else, where there were fewer buildings to fall, or where the population was not so dense.

I was out in San Francisco a week after the big earthquake of 1990 and I told people there that the earthquake itself did no harm. How many people go to bed and stay in the same position all night without moving? Sometimes you turn to the left, turn to the right, and roll over. Our Mother's been in the same position for many years, so she shifts, but the shifting itself does not hurt anyone. Only the manmade things hurt us—slabs of concrete, collapsed highways, broken water mains, and gas lines.

Many people were hurt on San Francisco's Nimitz Highway when that earthquake came. In the building of a highway, I just can't picture an engineer giving an offering to this Mother Earth and saying to her, "I've been commissioned to build this structure on your face here. We're going to use it in a good way, to help people get to work and to their homes. I offer just this little token of respect to you for the privilege of building it." That's the way my people were taught to do things. That's our way of communicating with the earth. I don't see an engineer doing that when he's got so many dollar signs luring him to sign his name on the dotted line. I can't see an engineer or a commissioner of highways even think about giving an offering.

Multiply that situation all over the world. Where is that respect? Where is that acknowledgment? *My people were told a long time ago, "The rivers and streams are the veins of the universe. They're your lifeline, take care of them."* Today it's hard to find good clean water anymore. We've been very poor stewards of all that was given to us in its pure form. Instead we have become exploiters and abusers of the very thing that sustains our lives, and we think we have nothing to learn from the world around us.

LEARNING FROM OUR RELATIVES

In this scientific world of ours, we are continually making technological advances. Yet there are still things we can learn from our environment, even as our old people learned from observing animals.

Many yoga exercises were developed from the observation of animals. Watch a cat lying in front of a fire. It can be sound asleep, then all of a sudden it stretches and you can see the muscles rippling all through its body, toning up stored energy so that at a moment's notice the cat can be on its four legs, ready to jump. No matter what kind of work you do, sometime during the day take time just to stretch. And after stretching, see how good it feels to relax again.

The bear happens to be my father, because my dad was of the Bear Clan. There are different types of bears. The black bear can climb trees easily. Grizzlies are too heavy to climb trees, but very strong, and their intelligence is amazing; they can almost read your mind. A bear can come into a camp and then waddle off, just a few steps and it's gone. Where did it go? It's almost as though it knows how to become invisible. As a rule, bears that live in the forest, as big and clumsy as they look, are as gentle as they are strong—they can run through the forest and not break one twig.

Bears have many qualities we can learn from. The companies that make solar panels, for example, are now studying the fur of the polar bear because it is the best example of solar heating there is. Although the polar bear appears white to us, its skin and fur are actually colorless. There is no pigmentation in a polar bear's fur, so when it's hit by sunlight it appears white. Every hair is a hollow tube that retains the heat of the sun. That's why the polar bear is able to survive in subzero weather—it has a solar heating system in its fur. Just when we think we have reached the end of our knowledge in some particular field, something like this always comes up, so it stands to reason that there is much yet to be learned from nature.

The polar bear seems to understand that it must appear white to go unnoticed in the snow. When it hunts game and gets close to its prey, it will lie motionless, squinting and using its front paws to cover its nose and mouth because they're the only black spots on it.

Bears have their own system of communication. Mostly they use telepathy to communicate, but in an emergency they have a guttural sound they make to get attention, similar to our yelling, "Hey, hey, everybody, look, look," to bring attention to an urgent situation.

By nature, bears are very playful, even when they're hunting or fishing. When they fish, they're not fishing to make a living, they fish in order to live and, in so doing, make a game out of it for enjoyment. This is something humans can learn from. Even though you need to work to survive, don't let yourself get into a rut. After a weekend, Monday comes around real quick and you're driving yourself with everything you've got in order to get to your place of employment, just dragging yourself there. Somehow you lost the joy and appreciation of working when there are so many others who can't even find work. Where is your gratitude? *So if you have a job, and the job has become a rut, think of it not as an end in itself, but as a springboard to something else that will come to you. For the time being, make the most of it.* Work on your attitude, find the joy—just as bears make a game of fishing, trying to catch fish in a clear stream. They fish with their paws and make it a joyful experience.

There is much more that we can learn from bears. They travel long distances, looking for honey and berries. When a bear goes into a new territory looking for food, it looks for a prominent tree, one where the local bear has made its mark by standing up on its hind legs, reaching as far as it could to put its claw marks on that tree. The newcomer will stand on its hind feet to see how it measures up to that mark. If its mark is a little higher, then the local bear will have a problem—it will know that it's up against a bigger bear. Without fighting, it'll know it has to look for another area. So why do humans feel that they have to fight over their differences? Even the animals have a way of resolving competition without confrontation.

All animals have their own system of communication, whether we understand it or not. The dolphins have a system of communication, as do seals, even birds and trees. It has been proven scientifically that trees communicate with one another, even as far as fifty yards apart. If there's a damaging bug on one tree, that tree sends a message to neighboring trees so that when the bug arrives, a bitter substance has already been secreted into its leaves to discourage that bug from getting on it. There is such a close relationship among trees that when one dies, neighboring trees often die—there's a chain reaction.

Communication of the earth's creatures is all around us. Honey bees send out scouts to look for food. When the scout locates food, it comes back to the hive and does a particular dance. After that dance, the rest of the bees come out of the hive and fly to the exact spot where the food was found. Researchers have monitored the scouts as they located the food and, while the scout was returning to the hive, the researchers took the food and put it closer to the hive. But the bees flew over the food to the exact spot where it had first been found. So it is not a sense of smell that leads them to the food—it's the communication of the scout.

The coyote is a survivor. It's almost impossible to eradicate coyotes. People can poison other animals, but they've been unable to poison the coyotes—somehow they sense not to eat anything with poison in it. In Phoenix, Arizona, housing is spreading out northward from the city and the people complain that the coyotes are invading their property. But it's the other way around. The people are invading the coyotes' land. That's where they've lived for centuries and we're pushing them aside. But the coyote survives. We don't know how they live and make it in this day and age, but they do.

KEEPING THE LAND SACRED

Los Angeles is called the "Land of Sunshine" but it's been a long time since I've seen a clear sky in the California area. What happened? It's the manmade things we put on this planet that dim our view of the actual beauty that exists.

How does the ozone layer affect us? The hole in the ozone layer affects a one-cell organism that grows in the northern waters. When it begins to die out, that death breeds other deaths, including plant life that feeds the fish, on up to the whale. They will be gone in time. Everything on the earth is interdependent.

If our knowledge were represented by the radius of a circle, as we increase our knowledge the circle becomes larger. What's beyond the circle is the unknown, so that the more we know, there is more that is unknown, and it goes on that way. We're on the way to destroying ourselves. There's a great sand dune in Colorado and parts of Kansas and Nebraska that is growing, and with all our technology we don't know how to stop it.

Ten thousand pounds of junk mail are sent out every year. If 100,000 people refused junk mail 150,000 trees would be saved. Trees hold the soil together, and now their numbers are dwindling. When I was a boy we had no refrigeration out in the country, so we hung our water bucket on a tree limb with a gourd dipper in it. Even today, you can purify a bucket of water by hanging it in a tree for a day with cheesecloth over it to keep debris from falling in. You can take the water to any lab and have it tested—there will be no bacteria in it. Something about the tree purifies it. Most of my tribe always hung their water buckets on a tree limb outside. They might not have known exactly what it did, but they knew that it helped.

So often money distorts values. The Black Hills of South Dakota contain minerals that have great monetary value. Mining companies want to mine there, yet the Lakota elders view the mountains as sacred, just as the Vatican is a sacred place for all Catholic people. Many great leaders went to the Black Hills and fasted on vision quests. It's sacred land and the elders want it to remain that way.

The Black Hills were claimed by the United States government over one hundred years ago, but the courts recently ruled that no compensation was ever given to the Indian people for the taking of the Black Hills, so until compensation is given, the United States has no legal claim to it. The government now wants to reimburse the Lakota for the Black Hills so it will have valid ownership and can then turn around and sell or lease the land to the mining companies. The elders don't want compensation—they want the land returned. It's still unresolved today. Can you imagine tearing down the Vatican to mine for uranium? Yet that's what these mining companies are asking when they want to buy the Black Hills.

Many Eskimos were paid money for the right to run the pipeline over their property, and overnight they became rich. They were told, "This money is going to help you." Yet some of the Alaskan Indians did not know how to use that money, and as a result, many of the Indians who were suddenly rich became alcoholics and lost sight of their traditional teachings and talents. Money is not the answer to everything.

We were always told to respect the land. Each blade of grass, every leaf, even one pine needle, is trying to filter out some of the pollution that we cause. All of these things help make air breathable and life more comfortable for us, yet modern society seems to go along without much regard for them.

It's nice to have air conditioning. It's nice to have a refrigerator. But when freon escapes, it adds to the problem with the ozone layer. We don't see far enough ahead. We have scientific knowledge, but not the wisdom to guide that knowledge. As a result, we have what happened at Three Mile Island. We had the knowledge to contain a great power within those walls until radiation leaked. We didn't have the foresight to consider what to do in the event of leakage and the land is still contaminated today.

We have much to learn from nature if we would open our minds. We need to get in touch with our universe, to get in touch with the meaning of all that surrounds us. Until we get back in touch and in tune with nature, we're destroying ourselves.

I took a trip to Alaska not too long ago to speak primarily to the missionaries. They were telling the natives that practicing their traditional ways was the devil's work and that they would go to hell if they continued. I had a lot of fun with the missionaries. I told them that most natives didn't know anything about hell until the missionaries came, yet the missionaries seem to know all about it. It sometimes makes me wonder if it's because that's where they came from.

I encouraged the natives to talk about some of the knowledge that they had before they got all mixed up by "civilization." The natives said, "Progress has finally hit our island. We're educated. Do you see any igloos? No, we have bungalows. They're not properly insulated and we get pneumonia every year, but we're educated. We don't have dog teams pulling our sleds around anymore. If you got caught in a blizzard and you had your dogs, a good lead dog could always find the way home. And if things went from bad to worse you could always circle your dogs around you and sleep in the middle to keep warm. You can't do that with a snowmobile, but at least we're educated."

Another sign of progress can be found among the Osage people. When a tribal member died, after performing a ceremony, they would put the deceased in a sitting position and pile rocks right up to the head. That way, the deceased could be seen by the Great Spirit and not be lost in the ground. The sitting position is also like that of a fetus about to be born—it facilitates the deceased being reborn into the spirit world.

Many years ago when the Osage didn't know anything about diabetic comas, it appeared that one of their elders had died, so they buried him in the traditional way. Apparently he came out of that coma by himself, because that evening he came home looking very pale. It seemed strange, but his family didn't say anything other than to welcome him home. A few days later he seemingly died again. So they went through the ceremony a second time, put him back in the sitting position, and piled up the rocks. Same way, that evening he came home.

Some time later, someone asked the family, "Did he finally die?"

"We don't know, but the last time he pulled that trick,

we buried him the white man's way and he hasn't come
back yet."

So I guess that's a sign of progress.

*We've miscommunicated with our environment for a long time,
not knowing its language.* We've complicated things with our
great intelligence—we've created all this pollution, the hole
in the ozone layer, and the greenhouse effect because we're
so smart. Now it's time to get back to basics.

THE FOUR DIRECTIONS

There are still ways we can communicate with our environment and receive help. Passing on my training in the use of
herbs and chants would not be of value to you because the
kinds of herbs I use may not grow where you live and songs
cannot be learned from a book. But there are traditional
teachings that you can use, things that we all have in common. First of all, we're human beings. We also have the sunlight, the directions, and this earth and sky. We make use of
all these natural elements in the art of healing.

We are told that at night, when all is dark, it is difficult to
walk through the forest. We might trip and fall, step off a
cliff, or hurt ourselves in some other way. But when the sun
comes up we can see where we are going, so the sun represents knowledge, and this is why we call East the direction
of enlightenment.

*If you have a problem that you have no answer for, you can
face East and think about it and an answer will come to you.*
What is actually happening? There are two planes of the

mind. One is the conscious awareness, and right below that is your unconscious. The unconscious is the storehouse of every bit of knowledge you've ever received from the time of your birth, and it relays answers to your problems to your conscious awareness. So actually what you're doing by facing East is tapping into that unconscious knowledge so that you might know where to take that next step.

You can turn to the South if you have lost someone who's very close to you, a relative or a friend. South stands for the destiny of all mankind. In my tribe it is said that we come from that direction when we are born—we come into this life on the red road and we walk the four quadrants of the universe. When it comes time for us to cross over to the spirit world, we take the blue road to go out—blue represents spirit. There's also a red and blue mentioned in the Book of Revelations—it says that in the last days, the sun will turn blue and the moon will turn red. When we get to that blue road, there's a white bird that looks after us and keeps our way clear so we won't stumble. And the Wind People come along and push the soul across into the next world so that the deceased will not be roaming around but can find rest and peace. That's been our teaching.

Maybe you know someone who has passed on and you could never resolve it in your heart, it still bothers you. You want to make a clear path so that that person's spirit will go on and you will feel good about going on with your life also. *If you have lost a loved one and spend a lot of time on that loss, face South and ask for help to keep going on in life.*

West is the direction of gratitude. When the sun goes down in the West, it's the benediction of another day. *At the end of each day, stand facing West and say, "Thank you for all the things that happened today, the good as well as the bad.*" Why be grateful for the bad? Because there was a lesson in it. Try to find that lesson and grow from it. If you let difficulties bother you all the time, you're building a wall around yourself. Happiness is on the other side and inside is misery.

And sometimes you get to crying. You cry and cry and cry. If you're going to cry, cry for something. Don't just cry for crying. If your tears are coming out, if you have nothing else in mind, then think about this: you are cleaning your eyes so that you can see the truth a little better, so that you can see beauty, you can see something of a positive nature. Go ahead and clean your eyes out, then dry them and go on with your life. We learn from tragedy—we don't always know how much we value something or someone until they're gone.

We look to the North for emotional, physical, and mental health. We may have a loved one who's ill, or perhaps we're sick and want to get well. Lay down on this Mother Earth with your navel toward her and your head to the North. We can still receive healing energy from this earth. People talk about healing Mother Earth, but there's no one powerful enough on this planet to heal Mother Earth—we can help to preserve and replenish some of the good things on Earth, but to heal her, that's something else. She continues to heal us and give us energy.

You may have heard of the great warrior Crazy Horse. His Indian name was actually Prancing Horse, but the closest English equivalent was "Acting Like Crazy," so the translation came out as Crazy Horse. He used to stand barefoot on Mother Earth for hours at a time to get his energy going. If you're in a three- or four-story building it will take a little longer for the energy to rise up, but in time it will reach you.

It's still Mother Earth because Mother Earth gave us this wood, these bricks, and this concrete. Everything that we have—what we live in, what we wear, eat, and drive—came from the Earth, and we can still get energy from her.

So lie there with your head toward the North. In the North sits the bald eagle, whose head is white like the snow. The white of snow represents purity, and when snow comes we say it covers your path. If you have had difficulties in your life, all that's covered up—you begin to feel good and sound again and you can make new tracks.

12

A DIFFERENT KIND
OF CHURCH

THERE'S AN OLD STORY ABOUT A BABY GIRL BEING BROUGHT home from the hospital and her four-year-old brother asking the parents, "Can I be alone with her for just a little while?" The parents said, "Not right now, but a little later you can." The next day he asked again, so they put an intercom by the baby's crib, turned it on, and said, "Now you can be alone with her." The four-year-old went up to the crib and said to his baby sister, "Tell me about God. I'm beginning to forget."

The Scriptures say, "A little child shall lead them," and we say that children came here to teach us—to teach us how to be humble, teach us how to be forgiving. If you get after a child, the child cries, but later on he forgets about it and comes back and sits on your lap. Adults don't forget so easily—we carry around old hurts and pains. What are we going to do with them, have revenge in our hearts until the day we die? We have a tendency to forget how much we owe to the Creator. We seem to forget about Him when the sun shines in our lives. We forget until the dark times come and then we say, "Please help me."

Churches were never made for perfect people. That's why people go to churches, to draw upon the perfection of the Creator to enable them to walk a few steps further in this life.

THE RED ROAD

During World War II a question was asked as to whether the enemy we were fighting prayed to God. If they're praying to God and we're praying to God, whose side would God be on? If we're praying to the same God, we're both on the same side in the Spirit.

So if you're religious you can expound on theology and quote the Bible, but then there's another aspect of living this life, and that's the path that Native American people call the "red road"—the road that leads to life, the road of spirituality, the spirit road. How do we become spiritual? By having an experience of oneness with the Great Being. We can't understand it and we don't try to analyze it—it's a feeling in our heart and soul that inspires us.

I have been asked what God Native Americans pray to. There is only one living God, but there are many ways, from many cultures, to contact the same God. People sometimes refer to idols as "God" but idols are inanimate. I am referring to the "living God." In the Old Testament, Elijah had a contest with the people who worshiped the idol Baal. He said, "Let fire come from your God, and if it doesn't, it will come from mine. You first."

They built an altar and went through their chants, rituals, and dances calling on Baal. And there was Elijah whooping it up: "Maybe you need to call a little louder, maybe he's asleep and can't hear you." Nothing happened and finally they gave up. Then it was Elijah's turn and, just to make things more challenging, he doused the altar with water four times. When he called on God, the altar flamed up because Elijah worshiped the living God.

So the living God is one God. There are many ways people worship God, and that's why there are so many churches of different denominations—their rituals are different, the order of services are different, but it is the same God. Whether you go to a Catholic church, a Jewish temple, a Protestant service, or a Native American ceremony, if you are strong in your belief and your faith, you don't have to fear what anyone else does.

Native people have always recognized the living God, only we didn't know him as "God." In our languages we have our own names for the Creator, but the word *God* leaves us cold because we've read of the God of Vengeance in the Bible, a term that connotes fear. In Native American languages we say things like "He Who Gives Life" or "The Great Mystery." In the Creek language we called Him *Ofunga*, meaning "The One Who Oversees All Things." The Christians of our tribe now call *Him He-sah ketah nese,* "The Master of Breath." Whatever name we use, there's a feeling of warmth and closeness. If I'm in pain or need, I just call on His Holy Name and He's the one who's going to understand me; He's the one who's going to help me with my needs. That's the kind of relationship that we have when we call upon Him with these names.

The missionaries thought our Indian people worshiped trees, eagles, the Pipe, and many other things. We didn't then and we don't now—we are monotheistic. But we do acknowledge these things as gifts from the Creator, put here to help us. When we use herbs such as sage, cedar, and sweetgrass, we're not worshiping these items—we're using them to create an atmosphere where we feel comfortable addressing the Creator, whether we're in need of help or just want to adore His presence.

Part of our respect for the eagle stems from the fact that if a human looks at a mountain, he will see only one side, but an eagle can see both sides because it flies higher than any other creature and has very keen eyesight. *Since the eagle flies close to the Creator above, we ask that it carry our prayers to Him.* We can certainly pray directly to the Creator, but using these mediums through which our messages can be conveyed shows respect because there are many people calling upon Him night and day. We, in our humble appeal, ask others to help us in conveying our message to Him.

We might have a loved one far away who is ill, so we use the Four Directions, the Wind, to carry our good energies to them. It is the living God who makes it possible for us to feel, to sense, that we are being thought of. At all times we keep ourselves humble because we're here to help our loved ones. If we can't be there in person to hold their hands and speak to them, we can still leave them in the capable hands of a living God who can help them.

Before we had the Sacred Pipe, we would touch a tree to connect to the Creator, who created both the tree and our lives. If we lived in an area where there were no trees, we'd take dirt and do the same thing—touch it and then touch our bodies with it. It's not the dirt or the tree, but the Creator who made them that we were honoring. Colors, fetishes, and the Four Directions are not gods in themselves. They represent that which is powerful, our medicine way—the Creator put them here for our use and they provide a sense of having a ready connection with a Higher Being. So the answer is that there is only one God, not many gods.

THE SPIRIT PLACE

Many Native American tribes have a ceremony known as the Sacred Stone People's Lodge, more commonly referred to as a "sweat lodge." It's a purification ceremony in which stones that have been heated in a fire are brought into the lodge—the door is closed and hot steam is created by pouring water on the stones. As a result of that heat, we perspire and get rid of many of the toxins we carry within us. A sweat lodge ceremony is not an endurance contest to see how much heat you can stand. It's a place to communicate with the Creator.

The steam that rises from the stones is referred to as the "Breath of Spirit." In the Lakota language, the name for the sweat lodge is *inipi*. *Ini* means "spirit" and *pi* means "place," so its name is "spirit place"—the place where we communicate with a Higher Being. You've heard the word *tipi*: *ti* is "to live," so *tipi* means "to live place."

The sweat lodge is a sacred place. Even though we don't call it a church, we pray, think, and act as if we were in a church, that's how sacred it is. It is sacred in its construction—prayers are made when we dig the dirt out to form the pit for the stones and when we build the frame of the lodge from saplings. *It is said that when you are in a sacred place, you yourself will become sacred.*

It is an old-time way that our people tried to communicate with a higher power. We didn't have formal churches, so we tried to make contact the best way we could, by purifying ourselves first. We say we want to come before the Great Being with "clean hands," meaning a clean attitude, a clean heart, a clean life, as clean as we can live it. That's why many of our ceremonies involve fasting and sweating so as to appear before the Great Being clean inside as well as outside.

We can go to a sauna and sweat and perspire all we want to, but it's not the same thing—when we come to a sweat lodge, there are prayers involved. There's a cleansing, not only of the body, but of mind and soul. Just like being born again, we erase our past mistakes and heartaches and disappointments, sweeping them clean so that when we go out, we will make new tracks.

How do we communicate feelings to a Higher Power? The secret is humility. When we come into the lodge, the opening of the doorway is so small that we must crawl through that door on our hands and knees. That's the first lesson right there—humbling ourselves before the Great Being as we come in.

In the circle of the sweat lodge, we first bring in seven stones that have been heated in the fire. One is for the Creator, one for the Earth, four for the Four Directions, and one more for all living things. So when we sit there, we are in a little universe. And in that little space, we can pray for any situation on our planet, we can add our love, our concern for the good of the whole world. There are many things that we can pray for from our churches and our little lodges and it doesn't matter how great or small the structure because the One we appeal to has the greatest power of all.

Some people have hang-ups about praying. There's a story of a little boy who got an inspiration to pray and he started out, "God, I thank you for the beautiful mountains, the trees and the grass . . ." That's as far as he got. "God, I have so much in my heart that I want to say, but I don't know how to pray. I do know the alphabet, though. Listen real good, God, as I repeat the alphabet. Maybe you can put it into words and make a beautiful prayer from this alphabet."

Even if we don't know how to pray we can still communicate what's in our hearts to a Great Power. Although He already knows how we feel and what our situation in life might be, it's best to acknowledge it ourselves and say, "This is my situation. I need your help." And we're going to get that help in some way.

It's good to come right to the point when we pray. In the lodge we are told to say it and that's it. We're not out to impress anyone. When I'm conducting a sweat lodge ceremony, I tell people not to make their prayers too long because "you're going to have to walk with those prayers when you go out of the lodge. If they're too long they might snag on something and you'll trip on your own prayers. Make them short enough so you'll remember what you prayed for. Then you back up those prayers by how you live outside of the lodge and things will fall in place for you."

Prayer is a matter of communication from our heart to the One who's going to listen regardless of our station in life. We're praying to the Creator who understands and loves us. Many times I've seen some of the old people sitting in one of our ceremonies, praying in their own language because they're very limited in English. They pray for people who have undergone disaster. When they hear of countries where little boys and girls were made orphans overnight they say, "Put a good thought in the heart of someone to pick up a little orphaned child and say, 'I love you. Here's some food. Here's a little doll you can play with.' " Their tears stream down as they pray for the future, for the good in people. We can pray for these things if we are spiritual. The spirit just works, it doesn't think in terms of distance, it doesn't think in terms of time.

THE HEARTBEAT OF THE CREATOR

On the altar outside the sweat lodge is what many today call a pipe rack. We rest the Sacred Pipe against it until we're ready to smoke it in the lodge. The elders taught that it's not really a pipe rack—it's half of a burial scaffold. Instead of burying their dead, some tribes put them on a scaffold so that nothing comes between the body and the Creator. Half a scaffold shows that we here on this planet are cognizant of the world above, and so we use half of the scaffold to rest the Pipe, which reaches between here and the other world.

When we use a drum, we're aware of the spirit inside. Symbolically, everything that gives life in the universe is represented inside the drum. The wood was once a tree that had life-giving substance flowing beneath its bark, just like blood going up and down our bodies. And the skin covering the drum was once life—it surrounded a body and there was life flowing beneath it. Both the skin and the wood were related to life that's gone on, yet they are helping the lives that are still here.

What this drum represents to us is a heartbeat. As we dance to the tempo of the drum, we are dancing in harmony with the heartbeat of our Creator, which is life. And as people dance together, we are all in harmony with our fellow man.

This drumbeat is a pulse, rather than a tempo; it's a life pulse. *If anyone is feeling great pain from a heart condition and you have nothing on hand to give that person, just beat a drum steadily while you are waiting for help.* The spirit of the One who gave us life, the Life Form of all life forms, is being called upon, and in time, that person's heartbeat is going to catch up with the drumbeat. You don't have to be a great medicine person to do this. You just have to have a lot of love in your heart to be able to do it, a lot of concern for your fellow man. That's why the drum is a sacred instrument to us.

Then there is the spirit of the fire. In our Indian way, we say the fire is the sun here with us. The sun shines on the trees for days, weeks, months, and years, and the wood absorbs that sunlight. Then the tree is taken down, and when we put a flame to it, that sun is now here with us in the form of fire.

We also say fire came to us a long time ago, so it's our grandfather. When that wood burns up it turns gray, like an old man, a grandfather, and we give it the same respect we give our elders. To be a fireman in our ceremonies is a position of great honor. Non-Indians have a fireman who puts the fire out. Ours starts the fire.

When a fireman handles the fire, he handles it very gently because he's handling an old person. He doesn't shove the wood around, because dishonoring the fire has its penalties—it can warm us, give us energy, and cook for us, but it can also burn us, our loved ones, or our homes. So we always respect that fire. We're very gentle with it, like an old person.

When our firemen put the flames out, they do it very gently. They don't just take water and douse it all at once. They do it very gently, because they're not putting the fire out, they're putting Grandfather to sleep. They're thanking Grandfather for helping us and saying, "Now, you've earned your rest. We thank you for helping us. There may be a time when we're going to have to wake you up again and ask you to help us. But right now, we want you to sleep."

The fire that burns in our fireplaces is the eternal fire, it is the sun here with us, lighting our way. Among the different Indian tribes, we respect the fire that way.

THE SACRED HOOP

Both the sweat lodge and the tipi are round—in fact, most Native dwellings are round. We even have a dance we call the Round Dance. A circle is without end—there's no time element to any part of it. When people come together in a circle, there's a spirit of oneness, a sense of sacredness that comes from inside us. The circle contains an appreciation, an acknowledgment, of all the created forces at our command if we so desire.

Our old teaching is that the universe is in harmony as long as we keep the Sacred Hoop intact. The Sacred Hoop is the circle of all life—the Four Directions, the Earth, and everything that lives on the Earth. It includes not only the two-leggeds, but also the four-leggeds, the wingeds, those that live in the waters, those that crawl on the earth, even the plant life. *Everything is part of the Sacred Hoop and everything is related. Our existence is so intertwined that our survival depends upon maintaining a balanced relationship with everything within the Sacred Hoop.*

So this circle represents the universe—it represents all of creation, united together as relatives. In our way of adopting a relative, we say, "Now your problems are my problems, and my problems are your problems." This is how we conduct ourselves when the Sacred Hoop is intact. As long as that hoop is intact, then we feel safe. But in this day and age, it's "every man for himself" and "survival of the fittest." The Hoop has been broken many times over because of man's disregard for his fellow man, the Earth, and those that live upon her.

What is the old "American spirit"? Why did the early founders of this country print on the dollar bill, "In God We

Trust"? Years ago, if a farmer's house burned down it would be put up again a few days later—all the neighbors would be there to help, to assist, to rebuild. The American spirit was that of helpfulness, of trying to live with common interests that served all the people. Then states were formed and governments expanded their role. Have we become too political? Have we lost touch with that which gives meaning to life?

Among our Indian people each tribe has teachings and values that children are taught as they grow up. If we abide by these principles, then we are keeping the Hoop intact. When we deviate from our early teachings and become full of greed, working only for ourselves without being sensitive to the needs of anyone else, especially our own people, we have broken the Sacred Hoop. Keeping that hoop sacred is not imaginary—that's where our Indian people and non-Indians differ a lot. Non-Indians may know our ways and do our ceremonies, but to catch the real true spirit of our teachings is to keep the Sacred Hoop intact and real in our lives. It is something tangible to our spirits.

In today's culture, the Hoop has been broken in many places. What we're trying to do is repair it. The circle brings us closer together. It's a place where we can come together in harmony with a sense of blending, forgiving, loving, tolerating. If we can live that way, then perhaps our world, which is the greatest circle, might be a better place.

THE ESSENCE WITHIN YOU

In my tribe, one doesn't have to be a medicine person to be authorized to conduct the sweat lodge ceremony. Above all, you must be well thought of within your community. After watching your life and your habits, the community must agree that you are the right person for it.

When there is a gathering in my community, if there are any elders around, the younger ones never say a word. I don't—even at my age, because I have many uncles and grandfathers back home in Oklahoma who are older than I am. In most places I travel to, I'm an elder, but when I get home, it's "Hey, sonny, come over here." If they're around, you won't hear a peep out of me, until they say, "Go ahead, grandson, we'd like to hear you speak to these people."

"All right, Grandfather, I'll do my best."

"Good, good, son. Go ahead." I have to acknowledge all my elders first before I even speak. That's the respect that we have.

When you're speaking to an Indian community, your gestures, mannerisms, presentation, and voice intonations mean nothing. The people sit with their eyes closed and listen for the ethos, the ring of truth and honesty, within you. Whether you're just talking or you're really saying something, they are asking themselves, "What kind of a life does this man live? Is this a person who backs up what he says by the way he lives his life, or does he just like to impress a lot of people? Is he a responsible man, able to handle groups of people like this?" By the time you get through talking, they know more about you than you will know about your audience.

Conducting a sweat lodge ceremony carries with it a lot of responsibility—you're responsible for everyone in there, their problems, their health, everything. Not only at that specific time, but in time to come. After the ceremony is over, you will still be expected to back up the prayer that you made in there for them. You back it up, not only with other prayers, but by the way you live when you come out of that lodge. It's quite a responsibility.

The elders taught us: "Before you can lead, have a home. That home is a base of operation, so that people know where to come and seek your help. If you're the kind that stays here awhile, and all of a sudden you're over there and people are trying to catch up with you over here, then over there again, your words, thoughts, prayers, and power are going to be like that—dispersed all over the place. You may go through the motions of leadership, but that's all—they're just motions. There's no substance to it, your character and habits are not solid."

Nokus Ele', or Bear Paw, the Seminole elder who put me on the anthill as part of my training, was a medicine man. A member of our tribe wanted to learn something from Bear Paw and extended an invitation to him: "I want you to stay overnight at my home."

So Bear Paw spent all night at this man's house, then got up early in the morning and waited until his host finally got up, too. The man said to him, "Breakfast is ready now, why don't you come and eat." In my tribe, people usually talk after the meal, so when they had finished eating, the host said, "I'd like you to tell me anything you think I ought to know."

"All right, I'll tell you, since you asked me," Bear Paw said, "because you want to live in the community and be well thought of. I saw a lot of your implements lying around in the front yard. Put them together in a shed so you can find them in one place. There are a lot of odds and ends all over, put those up."

What Bear Paw was telling him, in a nice way, was to clean up his act. And since he had asked an elder, the man couldn't talk back to him. Before you learn to do anything else, learn to keep your home in order and gain respect as a responsible member of your community, so that people will be glad to have you as a neighbor. That's the first lesson you need to learn. Until you do that, don't try to learn anything else. Your habits and behavior are what people know you by. If you sit in a responsible position, you carry that responsibility with you in your life. We don't put shingles out saying doctor of this and that. We learn by doing, by being. How do you keep yourself, how do you regulate your own life? When you give your word, do you live up to it?

I have a friend in Florida whose name is Billy Osceola, and he's a minister of the Seminole Independent Baptist Church. There was a non-Indian minister from Illinois who was visiting Florida, and he invited Billy to speak in his church. "When do you want me to come?" "Well, how about the first Sunday in April?" "Okay." This was in July, so it meant nine months off.

I was living in Oklahoma City that next April and I got a call from Billy as he was passing through. He said, "I'm on my way to Illinois. I'm going to preach for a friend I met from there." There had been no conversation or written correspondence of any kind since July, but Billy had given his word. A few days later he came back through Oklahoma City. The man who had invited him had forgotten. But Billy had given his word nine months before to go to Illinois and he lived up to his part of the bargain. He didn't realize that, in white culture, most people would send a confirming letter and see if the date was still on.

When Native people give their word, they don't have to have it notarized, they don't have to sign papers, and they don't have to confirm. That's why we as Indians call white

people the "paper tribe"—everything has to be written down
on paper. You need birth certificates, diplomas, and résumés
to prove who you are and what you've done. Reports must
be in triplicate—one goes to that office, another goes to this
office, another goes over to the bathroom. You see, it's a
waste. Give your word and live up to your word. That's the
kind of responsibility I'm talking about. It doesn't come
from books—it takes time, experience, and dedication.

There's a certain responsibility that goes along any time
that you are in a position to lead. It's as though everyone who
comes in the sweat lodge is saying to you, "I'm placing my
life in your hands. I'm giving you my life, will you help me?"
And so you are responsible for a whole armful of lives.

There was a big revival meeting one time and they brought
in an evangelist from out of state. A great deal of money was
collected and the deacons were going to turn this money over
to the evangelist, but one of the deacons said, "I don't know
whether we should give all of this money to the evangelist."

"Why not?"

"For one full week we've had only one convert. I don't
know whether we ought to give all of this money."

They were discussing this among themselves when one of
them said, "If it doesn't feel right, don't give it to him. But
whatever it is, I will match it and double it, because that one
convert happened to be my grandson and he's worth more
than that to me."

So how much is one life worth, a life that's entrusted to
you as you sit in a position of leadership? You're responsible for every soul, every problem. That's what that responsibility carries with it.

13

THE PEYOTE WAY

WHEN MY SON, MARC, DIED, I HAD BEEN PREACHING AT THE Otoe Indian Baptist Church for some time. I knew many people on the Otoe reservation and had been adopted by several families, so most of the reservation heard of our loss.

One cold afternoon a month after Marc's death, there was a knock on my door—three men from the Otoe tribe had come to see me. Each of them called me "brother" and they got right to the point: "You've helped our people. You've brought comfort to us all. When we've had deaths, you even shed tears with us, and we have great love for you. We want you to keep going on, to continue helping people, so to encourage you, we've decided to hold a tipi meeting and pray for you. You don't have to come to the meeting, you can stay out. Maybe in the morning you can come in and have breakfast with us. We'd like to cedar you off, send you good prayers, and try to keep you going. But before we put the meeting up, we have to have your permission that it's all right for us to do this for you."

I said, "It's very good of you to want to help me out like this. When you get everything ready and decide on the date, let me know and I'll come to that meeting. I'll be there from the beginning to the end." So I went to that all-night meeting and that was my start with the Native American Church.

THE NATIVE AMERICAN CHURCH

The Native American Church began around the turn of the century with a man named Quanah Parker, who was half-white and half-Indian. Quanah had great business acumen and owned many horses. He was also a good trader and a very smart man. He was converted to the Methodist faith, but from his traditional past he happened to have eight wives at the time he was converted. He was a strong man! I salute him. One day the bishop came to see him and said, "Quanah, you're going to have to get rid of all of your wives except one." Quanah thought for a long time and finally said to the bishop, "All right. You tell them." That's what I call smart!

Quanah's mother, Cynthia, was a white woman captured and raised by the Comanches in the late nineteenth century. Even though she was white, Cynthia had become a respected member of the Comanche tribe because she was gifted in many ways. When Cynthia's Comanche husband died, Quanah was still a young boy and the tribe told her that she and Quanah could go back to her people.

A short time after she and Quanah had returned to her family in Texas, Quanah got sick and almost died. The medical profession gave up on him, so, having been exposed to the Indian ways of healing, Cynthia went across the border to the Mexican Indians. She appealed to them to help Quanah and they came and doctored him with peyote. When he got well, he asked the Mexicans how they had cured him and they told him about peyote and how to use it. He said, "I'd like to take peyote back to my dad's people. They need something like this." So they made it possible for him to take peyote to the Comanches. This herb, which is viewed by the white culture as merely a hallucinogen, has been successfully used for centuries by Native people for healing.

After his conversion to Christianity, Quanah read the Bible and liked the teachings, but he didn't want to give up his identity as an Indian, so he went out by himself with dried peyote buttons so that he could chew them when he got hungry. When he got thirsty, he drank peyote tea. He fasted like that for several days, singing, praying, and reading the Bible until he received a vision. Finally he came back and told his people, "We're going to follow the Bible, but we're going to do it in a tipi. We're going to build an altar in the tipi out of this earth and we'll eat this peyote to cure our ills."

This was the forerunner of what is now called the Native American Church. It was formally chartered as a church in 1918 near El Reno, Oklahoma, with different tribal leaders attending. So it's not an age-old Indian tradition—it started earlier in this century.

The Native American Church was organized primarily to pray for people in need, be it physical, mental, or emotional. The church meetings are not held regularly and, with a few exceptions, there are no permanent structures to house the church—meetings are held in tipis and that is why they are also known as "tipi meetings." Whenever someone has a need, they sponsor a meeting, and even though the meetings are not held regularly, they sustain the participants on a daily basis because the experience of each meeting—the prayers, what people say—stays with them.

SOMEONE IN NEED MIGHT COME

In addition to praying with the help of peyote, the Native American Church is also based on Christianity and much of its symbolism reflects that foundation. The altar that Quanah shaped was in the form of a hoof print because he read that Jesus rode into Jerusalem on a donkey—the print of that donkey would remind the people of the King of Kings.

The top of the tipi has flaps, and when the flaps are open, it represents Christ hanging on the cross. If anyone needs help, they can come there. The poles of the tipi don't all come from one place—one comes from over here, another comes from over there—just like the people who enter the tipi. Their backgrounds may be different; people can trace their roots to various beginnings, but when they come together, they become as one. And when they enter the tipi, they have to bow down to come in, showing their humility before God Almighty.

Quanah read that the first man and the first woman had violated God's law and found themselves ashamed and that God took the skin of an innocent animal and covered their shame. So during the ceremonies Quanah had his followers use a kettle drum with water inside, covered by a skin. Using that skin in the tipi meeting means that none of us is perfect. "We have all made mistakes. Please overlook them. By using this skin You might forgive us." And they tie the skin to the drum by crisscrossing a cord over and under, back and forth, until it forms a star on the bottom, representing the star that guided the wise men and the shepherds to the birth of the Christ child in Bethlehem. This again represents the guiding star so that those in need of help might find their way to the tipi meeting. Seven marbles are used to tie it, representing the six days of Creation and a day of rest. The cord is never knotted at the end, it's just tucked in tightly, denoting the continuity of yesterday, today, and forever. Inside the drum is water and air, ashes representing the earth, and coal representing fire—the basic elements that give sustenance to this universe are right there inside that drum. And when we beat on that drum it represents the heartbeat of the Creator.

Then we shake a gourd as we sing. The gourd is round like the universe and the tassel is red like blood, representing the blood of Christ, who was crucified for mankind. The fringe represents our loved ones, and when we shake the gourd, the sound represents lightning, the natural element provided by God. By shaking the gourd, we're getting his attention.

We don't talk about the triunal godhead of the Father, Son, and Holy Spirit as such—we don't have to talk about Christ, but the spirit of His presence is felt just by using these instruments. We don't really talk about the Great Power and the Great Wisdom of God and what He can do. Instead, we talk directly to the Great Spirit from our hearts in our own way—we talk about our needs and the needs of our loved ones. That's how we communicate.

In our church meetings, we sing songs all night long. There is a word that Indians have always liked to use: *pitiful.* We have many songs that refer to our state of helplessness, and we wrap it up in the word *pitiful.* One of the Otoe songs says: "If there is anyone pitiful in this world, it's me. I feel as if I'm the most pitiful of all beings and I appeal to You for help. Bless me. Give Your strength to me in such a way that I can walk in a good way upon this land. In that way I come to You. Pitiful." That word *pitiful* is sung over and over again: *nah pede.*

In addition to the gourd and the drum, there's always a staff that is passed around the tipi with them. It's said that the staff represents the bow that allowed an Indian to hunt. It was his life, his security, sometimes his salvation when food was scarce. Our people say, "If you hold on to this staff, you can cope with life and walk through difficulties. It's up to you."

The staff also represents the staff of Moses. When Moses led the Israelites out of Egypt, Pharaoh sent soldiers after them. On one side were the mountains; on the other side were the desert and, just ahead, the great sea. He didn't know what to do, so he prayed and God told him to lift that staff to a horizontal position. When he did, the waters parted and the people walked across on dry land.

By holding the staff as Moses did, our people are saying, "Hold on to it, it's your life. You may have nothing left in life whatsoever, but as long as you hold fast to faith in a God who is great enough to overcome any obstacle, the way will be shown."

And in this church inside a tipi, we start in the evening and sing and pray all night and come out in the morning. In the Book of Genesis, it says, "Evening and morning was the first day." It doesn't say morning and evening; it says "evening and morning" were the first day. So we start in the evening and come out in the morning. At midnight, when a new day is beginning, the altar is swept, making everything clean and orderly. That means that whatever difficulties you might have had in life are now all swept away. In this new day you have an opportunity to make new tracks; it is now up to you to reach out and realize your own potential, assume your own responsibilities.

What is it that makes us the way we are? What is it that we are looking for in life? Have we been looking too long without seeing ourselves first? In the Native American Church the time before midnight allows you to see yourself. You see even those things that you don't like about yourself. After midnight you see your potential, the things you're interested in, whether it's art or engineering or something else. It might take all night, perhaps several all nights, but you're actually going to find yourself in there. *The fact that you take that time to sit up through the night when you could be somewhere else speaks for you, and in the morning you feel fulfilled; your mind and body have come together on a wonderful level.* When you get out, everybody is friendly; the fellowship is beautiful.

That was the early beginning of the Native American Church. It started out with the Natives and for a time they got real strict about not allowing non-Indians to come in. When they asked me for my opinion, I said, "If you want it all to yourself, call it something else, but not a church. Because when you add the word *church* to it, that's God's business there. It's His church and He created all people, so no human can take a stand like a God and say you can't come in." That's my feeling on it.

PEYOTE: A GIFT FROM THE CREATOR

Peyote, which is an important part of the Native American Church, has been used by the Indians of North America for a long time—about two thousand years. The Aztecs used to give it to their long-distance runners for endurance. Our Native tribes used it not only for clairvoyance—such as to find lost horses or an enemy camp—but also to heal all kinds of sickness. In fact, that's what it was originally used for.

Peyote contains more than fifty-seven alkaloids with kinesthetic, olfactory, and auditory derangement properties—it makes one highly sensitive. But scientists have determined it is non–habit forming and have also established its medicinal qualities. In one study, they injected twenty rats with a staphylococcus infection. Ten of them were also injected with peyocactin, an element found in peyote. Those ten survived while the others perished. That was just one such study on the healing properties of peyote.

When our Native people take peyote, they aren't concerned with what it contains—they don't know about alkaloids or any other contents identified in laboratory studies. Prayers are made not to the peyote, but in acknowledgment of the peyote as a medicine put here by the Creator to help the people. It is viewed somewhat like an aspirin, a cure for all kinds of mental, emotional, and physical problems. We don't take it to "get high" and we don't meet together for theological reasons. We come into the tipi because we need help, we need direction, we need strength and encouragement. Peyote makes people highly sensitive to sight and sound and more aware of what's around and inside them. It helps us in our worship of God and the communicants use it as a symbolic sacrament, much as the Christians use wine in the communion and the Jewish people use wine in the Passover celebrations. Our people say we don't hallucinate with peyote, rather we see visions that teach us.

Peyote still works for our people today. I visited an Otoe man in the veterans' hospital who told me that he had used it to see his son in action during the Korean conflict. He told me, "I was home on a Saturday, really worrying about my son. The heaviness in my heart for him was there. I didn't want to go to town because I'd just end up drinking if I did. So I stayed home and decided to take peyote and, in my own way, pray. I wanted to hear something good about my son, to see if he was safe. That's all I was asking."

So he ingested some peyote and closed his eyes. When he opened his eyes, he was flying and, looking down, he saw his son with a detachment of four or five soldiers who were surrounded by the enemy: "They were trapped and my son would have been trapped along with them, but I saw him crawling through the weeds and then the weeds seemed to give way and he fell into a dry creek bed that couldn't be seen because of the high grass around it. He crawled under a fence and got into some trees and made it to a safe area, so I felt good. I closed my eyes again and when I opened them I was still here lying in bed. I don't know how long it took, but I saw that."

He told this story to his wife. Two months later they got a letter from their son describing everything the father had seen. Exactly how he had seen it—that's the way it happened. The father could see all that by using peyote, and from that moment on he never took another drink.

THOSE THINGS BEYOND LOGIC

Those who conduct the Native American Church meetings are called "road men" and, much like the leader of a sweat lodge, a road man is responsible for all the people who come to the meeting and sit in that circle. He must be strong enough in character, knowledge, and wisdom to not only keep in mind the purpose of the meeting itself but also be able to handle the diverse problems of the people in that circle.

Until I became a road man myself, I never spoke in tipi meetings unless called upon, because there were almost always people older than I in there. One time a skunk came into a tipi while we were praying and most people in there started laughing and joking about it. I didn't join in, but instead became somewhat pensive. The road man was watching me and knew I had something on my mind, so he asked me to speak.

This was an adoption meeting—one of our road men of the Sac and Fox tribe had recently passed away and this meeting was for the person who was going to fill the space that he left. In our way, a person who is selected to take the place of the deceased must have qualities and characteristics similar to the one whose place he is taking within the tribe and family.

I said, "This skunk came in while we were praying. When you look at a skunk, he's a lowly being, something to be laughed at, something we'd just rather not have around. We make jokes about it. In fact, I know a real good joke about it.

"An old Indian was admiring a white man's dog. 'Boy, you sure got a good-looking dog.' The white man was getting ready to go somewhere and he was busy. The Indian asked, 'Would you like to sell him?'

" 'No, he's not for sale.'

" 'I'll give you a lot of money.'

" 'I said he's not for sale.'

"The Indian still wanted to have that dog. 'What kind of a dog is he?'

"This man, he's getting out of sorts with the Indian. 'Oh, he's half-Indian and he's half-skunk.'

"That Indian started to leave but stopped and said, 'Well, you take good care of him because he's related to both of us.' "

When the laughter died down, I continued to speak. "Now, think about the man who passed on—George Harris, my Sac and Fox father. When did you ever see him turn away a homeless person? When did you ever see an orphan go to his home and not leave with a pair of shoes or some food? He cared for those who others seemed to have abandoned in life. He even legally adopted an orphaned boy as his own son—he was that kind of a man. That skunk came in to emphasize the fact that this man who is to fill George's place within the family has to consider that even a four-legged like the skunk is a living being, created by the same Creator who created all of us. He has a right to live. It's the job of a road man to be able to see these things because he's responsible for everyone sitting around that circle. He must be sensitive to the needs of others and try to meet those needs."

We often speak that way in Native American Church meetings, reminding one another of how we want to conduct our lives.

We say peyote is "medicine," and many times our tipi meetings are viewed more as hospitals than churches because people get well in there by taking peyote. As a result, some of the road men are referred to as "peyote doctors." When someone is sick inside of a tipi, all the healing work is usually done after midnight, after the people have ingested peyote. This is also because, after midnight, we look toward the sun coming up and, symbolically, that sickness is going to be coming out of that person. Toward morning we sing a song we refer to as a "morning song" and the words say, "I will be well this morning."

When all is said and done, the belief system on the part of the one who's sick has a lot to do with recovery. If they believe strongly in prayers, that in itself can be a remedy, and they can get well. But sometimes they need assistance in that church atmosphere. Many people have been made well by peyote when M.D.s have given up on them.

There are many amazing stories told about some of the powerful peyote doctors of the past. One concerns a Ponca Indian who treated a lady who was very ill—she hadn't eaten for quite some time and couldn't keep anything down. She was just wasting away. After the peyote doctor had worked with her in the tipi meeting, she said she was hungry. So the peyote doctor told his fireman, "Go outside and you'll find an orchard to the south. Break a limb off the first tree that you come to and bring it to me."

So a limb was brought into the tipi. Because it was wintertime, the limb was bare. The peyote doctor stuck the limb right in the middle of the coals of the fire and said, "I'm going to sing four songs." As he started singing, leaves came on that limb, little buds. During the second song, little tiny fruit began to grow. With the third song, buds and leaves were all over the limb. By the fourth song, tiny little pears grew. He said, "Pick four and give them to this woman." So the fireman picked four and gave them to her. "Now, give one to each person in here." There were just enough for each person in that meeting. I know people who witnessed it.

Even today there are times when someone is really sick and, inside the tipi, we pray for their health. So we partake of that medicine on their behalf and as we take that medicine, we say to the Higher Power, "I want that sick person to feel as good as I feel when I take this medicine." We are speaking on their behalf and transferring good energy into them.

One Easter morning at my Otoe brother's place back in

Oklahoma, my Shawnee uncle was conducting a meeting. We'd been in there all Saturday night praying for my brother's granddaughter, who had a collapsed lung. She was diagnosed on Saturday morning at the Pawnee Indian Hospital but they couldn't take her in right away and told her to come back Monday morning.

Early Sunday morning, near the end of the meeting, my uncle brought her into the tipi. Cedar was put on the coals of the fire and she was fanned off with an eagle feather. She went around and shook hands with everyone, which is our way of saying thank you to each person. The next day, when she went back to the hospital and was reexamined by the doctors, they found nothing wrong with her; her lungs were fine. She wasn't even in the meeting and she didn't take any peyote, but those who were in the meeting did and they prayed for her and she got well. That's what I mean—things like that happen without any logical explanation.

If someone has a drug- and alcohol-abuse problem, we try to help them. When they come into our circle, we immediately take them as one of our relatives; we even call them "relative." Psychologically, that person's self-worth is lifted. There's a psychological benefit to sitting in a circle in a tipi— it's kind of like a mother hen, mother church. If you're from the country, you know how little chicks all gather underneath the mother hen when a storm is coming. They feel safe there. We find safety in the tipi itself. We feel that we're safe as long as we're there together.

In suffering, it seems as though we're drawn together. It's not easy to sit in a tipi all night long, on the ground. It's tempting to go stretch out somewhere because you're uncomfortable, especially after midnight. It seems like a long time just to be sitting there. The side of the tipi is slanted, so we're sitting at an angle. When we get up in the morning, we're kind of walking slanted forward. That's called the "peyote walk." And yet toward morning, the medicine that we've taken and the prayers that were said, the songs that we've heard and things that went on, seem to come together and we feel good. We feel like it was worthwhile going there, not only physically, but in our minds as well.

A non-Indian may get a computer or calculator and solve a math problem within a few seconds. Here's this old Indian trying to find that same answer by going "one plus one plus one . . ." It will take him awhile, but as long as he comes up with the right answer, that's all that matters. And that's what we do—it takes us all night to talk to the Creator about our troubles and our needs. As you're sitting there, whoever you are, you can be praying in your own way. There's no requirement that says you have to ingest peyote when you sit in a tipi meeting. They say that in a tipi meeting you're in a sacred place and, whether you pray audibly or not, your thoughts are in the atmosphere of prayer and every time someone puts cedar on that fire, the smoke carries your thoughts up as prayer. Maybe you're thinking about a loved one or some problems of your own. That thought goes out as a form of prayer. In the morning it's all going to come together and, when you go out, you'll feel like you've really been somewhere.

Those are just some of the things we think about when we appeal to this Great Being, when we make an effort and someone feels good from it. They thank us, but we were just an instrument, the healing went through us, but actually it came from Him. That's why we are reluctant many times to take credit because we really did very little and wish we could do more.

LEGISLATING THE GREAT SPIRIT

Recently a great dark cloud drifted over the Indian people who pray through the Native American Church. In the early 1980s, some employees of the state of Oregon were fired because they had been members of the Native American Church. They lost out on their retirement pay and every benefit they had earned through the years that they had worked.

We used to think very highly of our court system as a symbol of justice, but neither that judge nor the attorneys had ever been inside the Native American Church to see how that church is conducted. The case went all the way to the Supreme Court, and in 1990 the Supreme Court took away federal protection of religion and let stand an Oregon law prohibiting the sacramental use of peyote. How can they pass legislation concerning a church when the word *church* represents something that belongs to the Great Spirit?

We do not worship peyote. The Creator set it down here for our use. It's used for healing; it helps focus the prayers of our people who sit down on Mother Earth and talk directly to the Creator, praying for all mankind and for the little children not even born yet. That's what they've taken away from us when they rule against the very thing that we use in our church to help one another. Many other forms of worship can be affected by this one ruling against peyote.

There are many denominations, many disciplines that people practice. There are disciplines of meditation and disciplines of prayer. There are about seventeen kinds of Baptists and then there is the Methodist Church, the Pentecostals, and so on. It's like a big tree with a limb, and on that limb is a branch, and from that branch, way on the end, is a twig. And on the twig is a little knot—that represents our Native American Church. There are other big fine churches with majestic steeples, but ours is just a little place where you have to sit on the ground. But that little knot on the twig is part of that tree. It's not off to itself in outer space. *There's only one road that leads to the heart of God and that's the spirit road—that's what we strive to be on.* People tell me, "I've lost direction, I need direction for my life." I say, "Be sure you're on the path first before you start worrying about direction." When you find yourself firmly planted on that spirit path, then direction will come.

In the history of our country, we fought for freedom of religion. During the First World War, the greatest number of volunteers, proportionately, were the American Indians. We lost many of our loved ones—they paid for the freedom to worship anytime, wherever they please.

Faced with losing protection of our way of worship, people wondered what to do. We can write all kinds of letters, but we still believe in the omnipotent Great Being to intervene in such situations if we say, "Let a way be made so that there will be a continuance of the freedom of our Native American Church." We can call upon the Great Being, not only for ourselves but for all people, for all races. Especially for those who are coming after us, so that we can leave something everlasting that is good for all of mankind.

In 1995, the Honorable Bill Richardson, a New Mexico representative to Congress, introduced a bill calling for the Native American Church, and its use of peyote, to be accepted and protected by all the states. That bill was passed, so it demonstrates that our beliefs and prayers can be answered when we put our hearts and minds together.

14

THE SACRED PIPE

YOU MAY HAVE HEARD OF THE PEACE PIPE. EVERY TIME THE white men and the Indians would get together to talk about treaties or peaceful relations, the Indian way was to smoke the pipe first so the negotiations could be witnessed by the Great Spirit. The white man associated the pipe with the discussion of peace, and they are the ones who called it the "peace pipe," but to Native American people it has always been the "Sacred Pipe," an instrument for communication with the Creator.

BRINGING THE PIPE TO THE PEOPLE

Each tribe received the Sacred Pipe in a different way—the Pipe came to the Creeks many generations ago while we were still in Alabama. One version of the old story among the Lakota is that the Sun and the Moon are husband and wife and they have one daughter—the Morning Star. She's known as the "Most Beautiful One" and that's the only name she has. She was commissioned to be the one to bring the Pipe to the people and she came down as a white buffalo calf to make the presentation.

Although she came here as a buffalo, she then turned into a beautiful maiden dressed in white buckskin and carrying a bundle. Two men saw her and one had lust in his heart and mind, thinking about what it would be like to be with a woman like that. Able to read his mind, she called him over and, as he stood in front of her, a bluish whirlwind, a spirit wind, came and enveloped him. When the whirlwind stopped, almost nothing but bones were left, and his remaining flesh was eaten by snakes.

The other man had respect for her, so she told him to go and put several lodges together, big enough to gather all his people inside. "I have something sacred to present to the people. I will teach them how to use it and how to take care of it." In that way she presented the Sacred Pipe to the people.

ASKING FOR HELP

I have five Pipes. I have a medicine Pipe that I use for doctoring, an altar Pipe that I use when I run sweat lodges, a long-distance Pipe that I use for healing at a great distance, a working Pipe that is for general prayer, and a personal Pipe.

I use my personal Pipe if I'm asking for more strength in order to meet certain demands and needs. I once met a little boy born without arms who asked me, "Can God give me the rest of my arms?" I said, "I'd like to talk to you about it, but I'm quite busy right now, so we'll sit down and talk about it a little later." Knowing that it was not meant to be, that's when I used my personal Pipe. I wasn't going to doctor him, so I didn't need to use my medicine Pipe. I used my personal Pipe to ask for strength and guidance as to what I could say to help him accept his condition and still make the most of his life without feeling great disappointment. I knew how he saw other children playing ball, and how he missed things like that, so I had to rely on a Higher Power to give me the strength and wisdom to talk to him.

When I met with him afterwards, I said, "When we come into the world, there are many things God intends for us and He must have something very special in store for you in order to bring you into this life without your arms. As you continue with your schooling, you'll find something that appeals to you, something that you'll really enjoy. Seek out all there is to know about it, specialize in it. Perhaps that's the area you're going to excel in. Any number of opportunities will become available to you. There's a certain amount of disadvantage at the moment, but you're not disabled by any means. Today there are organizations that help little boys like you. They may have to give you mechanical arms so you can do things such as write and drive a car, but even now you can still think, talk, see, and hear. And with those gifts, you can make something of your life. So don't think about changing the way you are. Accept it by saying, 'This is what God intended for me. I'm going to make something of myself because He gave me other gifts—I can become anything I want to be.'"

So we talked that way. It wasn't an easy thing to do, to talk to a boy like that when he expects so much, but that personal Pipe helped me.

LETTING THE SPIRIT HAVE MORE OF US

We have been taught that the bowl of the Pipe represents the universe and the stem represents mankind, reminding us that we are related to all living things. And the tobacco that reaches the center of the bowl represents the Father of All

Creation, of All Wisdom, first in our lives as in the life of this universe.

As sacred as the Pipe is to us, we don't need it in order to pray. The Pipe neither adds to nor subtracts from the power of prayer. Power comes from on high and Pipe, beads, candles, incense, or anything that people might use in order to pray is meaningless if our heart's not right—if it's done for ego and ego alone, these things are nothing but trinkets. We must yield our life to the Greater Power, and by so yielding we may appropriate the power that comes from On High, and in that way we can ask for anything that we desire.

The form of prayer isn't important because whatever is in our heart can be relayed to God, but ritual gives us focus and direction. We know sunlight has the power to burn paper, but it doesn't. It's only when we take that paper and hold a magnifying glass to it, intensifying the sunlight, that the paper will burn. Similarly, the power of the Creator is all around us, but we don't often focus it on any specific area. When we focus that power, we may get a stronger feeling of accomplishment. As we see the smoke of the Pipe rise, we can almost see our prayer going up to the Creator, creating an atmosphere of prayer and encouraging us to pray. There are times in our lives when our prayers don't even seem to reach the ceiling because our spirits are so low—the Pipe helps keep our spirits high.

We must handle the Pipe very carefully because we're praying and talking to our Creator about our own lives and the lives of other people, infants as well as old people and those in between. The smoking of the Pipe is an appeal for healthy attitudes within a healthy body—that's what we ask for. And as we smoke we're not inhaling, we're not just smoking for enjoyment, we're sending our prayers up with that smoke—it's not the smoke that's important, but the communication that goes with it. Most of my elders were nonsmokers, except in ceremonial situations, and they told us to be careful when we smoke the Pipe, because there is a Witness to our thoughts and prayers. We don't smoke the Pipe to impress others—we smoke it because we have something in our heart and on our mind and we want to tell Him about it. The Pipe has a power of its own to wipe away our tears: "I will carry your pain to the One who can handle it for you."

REPRESENTING THE SACRED

There is an old teaching that how we carry ourselves in public, away from our ceremonies, reflects on that which we represent. We're not just out there by ourselves anymore. If you are a Pipe carrier—if you are committed to any spiritual path—you represent what is sacred. And this is not for a week or a month, this is a lifetime commitment.

There are many, many teachings that go along with the Sacred Pipe—qualities that a Pipe carrier tries to attain. The first is humility. It's hard to be humble because you can't brag about it—if you're really humble.

My adopted Otoe dad, Joe Carson, was of the Beaver Clan. The Beaver Clan picked out the campsites for the tribe as they moved from one place to another. "Here's one for the chiefs. The warriors will be over here. The medicine people over there. The rest over here." For themselves, they were always way out on the tail end. They always camped away from the rest of the tribe, where they could view the entire campsite. That way, if there was a need anywhere, they could attend to it. Even today, a member of this clan cannot be a chief. They can be medicine people or warriors, but they cannot take positions of leadership. They don't even speak in public unless someone asks them to. Their main function is to serve the people, and they look upon it as a privilege to be of service.

Joe used to say this: "The Beaver Clan serves the people and I am of this clan. But I was also an orphan and that wasn't easy. You stand in line to get food, but usually in the back. By the time your turn comes around, most of the food is gone. When you get hurt there's no mother or father to run to. It wasn't an easy life. I'm a poor man and when anyone does something for me, I am so grateful that when I say thank you, I say it in my Indian sign language." The sign language for "thank you" is lifting your hand with an open palm and making a motion of bowing down. "But me, I am so poor, I actually bow not only with my hand but with my body, all the way down and touch the ground. I'm that humble, I'm that pitiful, and I'm that grateful. I'm a nobody."

One day, he was sitting in a tipi in Red Rock, Oklahoma, and called me over: "Son, come here." I sat down beside him. "I want you to watch these coals." He went over to the fire, sang a chant, and put his hands over the coals. Then he picked up some coals with his bare hands and held them. "Watch this now." He cupped his hands with the hot coals between them and when he opened his hands a yellow hammer bird flew out. Still, he said he was nobody.

Joe was a peyote doctor in the Native American Church. If he was going to give medicine to a patient, he would chew the medicine, hold the fan of yellow hammer feathers in front of the patient's face, and spit the medicine into the patient's mouth by spitting through the fan. Next thing you know, it was in their mouth, without their even having opened it. He could do things like that, so if he's a nobody, then I'm a nothing compared to him. Just call me "nil."

To be truly humble is not an indication of weakness. If someone has lied about you or taken advantage of you, you may be filled with all kinds of answers that you could make, but it takes a greater strength to keep quiet. When someone says such things against you, maybe they are envious and don't want you to succeed in life. They want you to hear about what they're saying and lose your cool. Instead, we go to the Pipe, not for revenge, but to let a Greater Wisdom handle it, saying, "This is my situation. Only You can understand, so I offer this smoke to You and place this problem in Your hands with gratitude that You are here for me. I sit on Mother Earth so she may absorb my tears and bring me a sense of joy instead of hurt. I want to feel good, not only about myself, but about the person who said these things. Please take care of it." We've put it in Greater Hands, so it doesn't come around and nag us so much and in that way we become stronger as a person and worthy as a Pipe carrier.

When someone does speak against us, whether it's unfounded or not, there is a certain amount of damage done to our character. And if what is said is true, as a Pipe carrier, we will have the courage to own up to it. But if it is not true, we will still have the courage to talk to that person and say, "I heard that you said this, I take no offense. You felt in your heart that this was so and it's your privilege to think and to say what you want. But I extend my hand to you because, although I say it is not true, something caused you to say it, and that's going to make me watch myself more closely. You helped me with that, so I thank you." When we have the courage to extend our hand to that person, we help ourselves because we'll be strong enough to cope with any problem that comes up. And as far as our own conscience is concerned, we feel free.

So we walk with confidence, look people in the eye, and go on. In that way we're standing up for the Pipe, we're being loyal to that Pipe. They say, "If you stand up for the Pipe, in times of need the Pipe will stand up for you."

Our people also say that if you get angry you've lost the battle. Likewise it's said that, as a Pipe carrier, if we let anger get hold of our mind, our behavior is affected. Holding on to anger sometimes blocks that pipe stem and it can turn back on us. If we clog it up with negative feelings, then smoke can't even go through, and that's when our mind goes all kind of ways. We might live a clean life in one sense of the word, but we must also have a clean mind.

One of the great teachings of the Pipe is to always keep our pipe stems clean. The Pipe is a reminder of how our lives should be. When we look at the stem, is it clear? Likewise, is our life clear? Are we clear enough to make a request of the Great Spirit? Asking ourselves those questions keeps us humble because, as we hold on to the Pipe, it seems as if we are holding on to our own lives. We have to keep ourselves out of the way because we are instruments, channels. We keep the stem clean so that, on one end, man, and on the other end, the Creator, can make a communication. It's the same way in our lives—when we make a communication to others, we become channels.

The Pipe must be used in a positive way at all times. We must never ask for anything negative with the Pipe, and even if we are financially destitute, we don't use the Pipe to ask for money. We can make an appeal and say, "If you can work a way for me, I would like to meet my financial obligations. I have many." We're not directly asking for money, but to meet the needs that come up. And we don't make it a practice to use it like that over and over, we do it only when we really have need for it.

Another quality of a Pipe carrier is compassion. Many people want to be compassionate but don't know how. If someone comes to you and says, "I haven't eaten in two days," it won't mean anything to you if you've never been hungry in your life. But if you have gone without food for several days, as my people do on a vision quest, then you'll know exactly what that person is talking about. Then you can be truly compassionate.

An effective leader, if he's going to be of any great help to people, is also identified with his mate. What does the community think of her? Is she sharp-tongued, does she cut people off, attack them verbally, is she ready to strike at a moment's notice? Or is she an easygoing, compassionate, nurturing type of person? It's not written as a rule, but it's felt. Maybe the wife never says much but supports her mate in what he's trying to do. People feel that, sense that, because it's sincere. And anything that's sincere in godly things does not stay hidden. It begins to show itself in some way, some form.

Humility, courage, loyalty, compassion. These are just some of the qualities our people need to develop to earn the right to carry the Sacred Pipe. Among our Indian tribes, our leaders were not just those who were great warriors. The qualities expected of those who carried the Sacred Pipe were the same qualities we looked for in our leaders. Even today, leaders are meant to set an example, be role models for the young ones growing up. A leader must always keep in mind what is best for the tribe, not what is best for himself. A leader must be beyond reproach to hold on to the trust given by each voter who elected him to be that leader. He must not let them down. He must use what knowledge he has gained to bring about the betterment of the whole tribe, setting up programs in such a way that those who grow up in the next generation may have the benefits that will help them economically, socially, and above all, spiritually.

Those are the things that a good leader always has in mind. When our elders in the past prayed, they always prayed for those coming after them. Not "What's here now, what can I get from it?" but "What can I put into this so that it will be long lasting?"

The chief in the old days was the poorest man in the tribe. When he came back from a hunt he would give to the widows and the old people who could not go out and hunt for themselves. Wherever there was a need, he gave away willingly. He had very little for himself or his own family. That's how our leaders used to live—for the people, not for how much they could get for themselves. In the Bible two questions were asked to gain entrance to the Kingdom of Heaven: "When they were hungry did you feed them? When they were naked did you clothe them?" Our leaders could have answered those questions with "Yes."

TODAY IS A GOOD DAY TO LIVE

When we have an individual connection with a Higher Power, we feel protection as well as sustenance, encouragement, strength, and guidance. All of that is part of our relationship with our Creator, and we must always remember that we are not alone in anything we do. Whether we are at work or play, that identity with our Creator, with those things we believe in, goes with us.

In the old days, even the few violators of peace we had in our tribe exhibited strength of character and identification with the ways of our people. When our tribe was relocated to Indian Territory, we were allowed to maintain our own government and our own tribal laws that did not affect the white man. The law enforcement members of the tribe were called the Lighthorsemen—they were the ones who brought in people to be tried and punished. Our laws were very strict—incest, rape, and murder brought a death sentence. If someone stole something even as simple as a handkerchief, he was given ten lashes on his bare back. If he stole a second time, he received twenty lashes. A third offense would bring fifty. If he committed something beyond that, in the eyes of our people he had become a habitual stealer, so a fourth offense meant death. That's how we had enforcement among my people.

We had no jails, so if someone was sentenced to death, the judicial council would tell him, "When this tree casts its shadow on that rock two moons from now, you be here in front of it." Then he would be permitted to go home and take care of his affairs. The accused was allowed to name his executioner, and it was usually his best friend. On the designated day he would show up, without jail, without being forced or handcuffed. We didn't have to drag him back. He didn't take off running somewhere else; he had every opportunity if he wanted to, but he almost always came back and the friend would aim a rifle at his heart.

Before I was born, my half-sister's father, Jackson Knight, was called on to execute a friend. He couldn't sleep for days before the execution, but he had a job to do, to fulfill his friend's wishes. And the friend knew that there was no judgment on Jackson's part, no condemning. He accepted the fact that he'd brought this on himself, so he didn't hold Jackson accountable for his death. Yet still it bothered Jackson, and after the execution he said, "Allow me to put him away." He was the one who took his friend's life and he was going to see that he was buried with dignity.

When the accused appeared for his execution, he showed his identification with the ways of our people. He didn't want to make it look bad for his own relatives; he didn't want his children to hear people say, "Hey, your dad's a coward." That's how we kept up our laws and their enforcement, and we didn't have too much crime as a result.

This went on until Indian Territory became the state of Oklahoma in 1907, and then the laws of the white man governed all of us and they did away with executions by our tribal council.

Native people have a saying that they strive to "walk behind the Pipe." It means that they do their best to incorporate the qualities associated with being a Pipe carrier into their lives and that a commitment made while praying with the Pipe is, and has always been, sacred. Although the representatives of the United States Government also smoked the Pipe when peace treaties were signed, they apparently did not view the pledge made with the Pipe as sacred. More than 370 treaties were made between the United States and the Native American tribes, and the United States Government broke every single one of them.

George Armstrong Custer, famous for the Battle of the Little Big Horn, had an obsession with the Indians. An example of this obsession occurred while he was stationed at Fort Supply in the northwest part of Oklahoma. There was a truce in effect with the Cheyenne allowing them to live and hunt in that area. But General Sheridan was determined to eliminate the Indians, despite the treaties, and sent Custer to do the job. In the winter of 1867 to 1868, a small band of Cheyenne was camped on the Washita River under the leadership of Black Kettle, who had always sought peace with the white man. Under the terms of the truce, the Cheyenne were allowed to hunt during the winter for survival, so this was a hunting camp, and they had their women and children with them. The place was known as Horse Shoe Mountain, but it was more like a mesa in the shape of a horseshoe. It made a good camp because the mesa provided a windbreak.

When Custer's scouts located Black Kettle's camp, they reported back to Custer and he brought his troops in during the night. It was freezing cold and Custer ordered them not to make a sound, not to even light a cigarette that could be seen. They stayed on the north side all night. Early in the morning a woman gathering wood for her fire happened to look up and saw the soldiers silently coming in on both sides of the hill that surrounded their camp. She warned Chief Black Kettle, who, knowing of the army's history of unprovoked attacks on Indian camps, gave the order to retreat: "Everyone get ready and retreat, the soldiers are here."

By the time they started to retreat, the soldiers had surrounded them and started shooting. They shot Black Kettle's wife's horse, so Black Kettle grabbed her and put her behind him on his horse. As he raised his hand in a gesture of peace, the soldiers shot and killed Black Kettle and his wife. Only a handful of children survived that battle—most of the men and women were killed but, in the eastern newspapers, Custer was reported as a hero for wiping out a whole band of marauding savages.

This was an unsuspecting camp of peaceful Indians. During the attack, they had many opportunities to kill Custer, but they respected that truce because it was made with the Sacred Pipe. That's why they didn't fight back—they tried to retreat and they were murdered instead. That's how far the meaning of the Pipe goes for us, that's how sacred it is. There was a Witness above who saw the Pipe being used, saw the Cheyenne give their word, so they held true to it though their lives were taken as a result.

Custer and his men continued attacking Indian camps, killing as many as they could and raping the women. That's what got the Indians together. Too many of their loved ones had been slaughtered by Custer, and they decided to wipe him out. The Lakota, the Cheyenne, and other tribes left their differences behind and banded together and their military strategy is yet to be equaled.

In 1876, at Little Big Horn, Custer thought he caught their camp by surprise and attacked without waiting for reinforcements. The Indians appeared to retreat, so Custer said, "We've got them on the run," and fell right into a trap. There were other warriors in wait, and Custer and his men were surrounded. The battle became known as Custer's Last Stand, and every schoolchild has read about it.

What's not in the history books is that the Indians were instructed to take Custer alive and, if captured, he would have been tortured by the women. When the women got together and tortured a prisoner, it was real bad. They did things like put splinters in the genitals and set them on fire while the man was still alive. That was just one form of torture. There were a lot of things that women did, and they were mad enough to do them to Custer because he was responsible for the rape and murder of their loved ones.

The story among the Indians is that, knowing he would be tortured, Custer took his own life. As a result, the Indians didn't take his scalp. He was known as Long Hair because of his long, flowing hair, but Indians only took the scalps of enemies they viewed as courageous warriors—they left Custer alone because he was a coward in their eyes.

In that battle, the Indian warriors had an opportunity to fight until death because the reason for fighting was to take revenge for those who were victimized—women raped, children murdered or orphaned, the elders whom they loved shot down without opportunity to defend themselves. Throughout the day, the battle cry was "This is a good day to die; whether they kill me or not, I'm going to take some with me." It was that kind of a fight: "Don't hold back, don't stand back. We came here to defend our loved ones. It is a good day to die." This was the way they encouraged one another.

And so, with a historical past like that, because their ancestors did die, Native Americans today can rally up and say, "Because of them, this is a good day to live. This is a good day to continue with our ceremonies and share our spiritual values so that one day the white and the red who fought one another can truly live in a spirit of oneness. Let it be our battle cry everywhere, so that not only Indians but everyone can truly say, 'This is a good day to live.' "

15

BECOMING
A VESSEL—
THE VISION QUEST

AT ONE POINT WHEN I WAS GOING TO SCHOOL, I WANTED some extra money, so I went to a neighbor and offered to cut a tree stump out of his yard. Boy, it seemed easy to cut wood in those days! But after I hacked away all the roots and dug around the stump, I still couldn't budge it. After a while, an old farmer came along: "Hey, sonny, what are you doing there?"

"I'm trying to remove this stump."

"Well, did you cut the tap root?"

"What's that?"

"That's the middle root that reaches down deep into the earth. That tree has one, and as long as it's there, you can't move it."

When I cut it I was finally able to remove that trunk, but as long as that tap root was intact, it couldn't be moved.

In order to be upright, solid individuals, we need to send our roots deep into the source from which life comes. If your life is built on something solid, the winds and the storms of life may blow, you may sway back and forth, but you will stand strong as long as you firmly hold on to that life-giving force.

SITTING BULL

You may have heard of the famous Hunkpapa Sioux chief, Sitting Bull. The name Sitting Bull referred to a bull buffalo sitting on the crest of a hill—not because he's tired, not because he's given up, but rather, because he sits looking at where he has been and what he has meant to others. He was revered by the Indian people as the source of their survival—food, clothing, and shelter. To non-Indians he was sport, driven to the brink of extinction. He looks back on that history and, after looking back, he turns and looks toward the future.

There is always a point where it's beneficial to stop and take stock of our lives, to look back and assess all the experiences that got us this far, asking, "What have I learned, how can I use these experiences to enable me to keep going forward?" Everything we've experienced—including the hurts, disappointments, and frightening times—had a part in shaping us and showing us what we're made of. Sometimes we have been driven to our knees in despair—there were times when we didn't know whether there would be another day or not because the situation was so bad, so devastating. We may have felt like giving up because it seemed as if there was nowhere to go, no one to talk to on this planet. We build up many attachments that may need to be blown away by the tornadoes of life, leaving us a clear path to travel on. It doesn't matter how physically frail we might be, there is a power inside that gives us the strength we need to keep going forward.

So, like the buffalo, sitting down and assessing, that's where this great Indian Sitting Bull received his name. You can't walk or run all the time. Sit down occasionally and see your surroundings. If you go in and out of a house every day, there may be one particular blade of grass on the lawn that always stands there watching you go by, but you don't even notice it because you're preoccupied with getting to work on time. You're thinking about the traffic, you're thinking about the day ahead—"When I get to the office I'm going to do this and do that"—and you miss the little blade of grass that stands as a protector, trying in its own way to filter the air so we can all breathe better. The grass and its relatives are beneficial to our bodies, so next time you rush out, stop, look down, and say thank you before you go on. It's an injection of joy and beauty into your life. That little blade of grass has life just as we have life. *Sit down and notice the world around you.*

If that sitting bull could talk, what would he say to us? What would he teach us? He has great strength, he's a leader of the herd. They're under his charge and he's responsible for their safety. And he looks, not only back, but to what lies ahead. In my heart and mind I think there were times when he looked up to those who went before him. Who has played a part in your life that has made you what you are today? As you look back, who was there helping you? I talked about my mother starting me off as an infant. There have been many, many people involved in my life. *Our lives become more meaningful when we remember those who went before us.* They made a way for us and we're grateful.

Like the sitting bull buffalo, the bear also takes time for assessment and rejuvenation. He eats enough during the year to sustain him during the winter. In hibernation, he's resting all over, not only his body but his whole being, while he's safe and warm in his den.

Likewise, in my tribe, we prepared for the winter before cold set in. If we had any livestock we butchered them and put them up in a smokehouse and we stored up our firewood.

We were more or less all set for the winter, so it was a time to slow down and contemplate, to review the past year and consider how things will be in the coming spring. We made plans and enjoyed the moment, friends and family came to our homes and we talked things over. Among my people, it was the time to tell our legends and laugh a lot. For a while we stopped beating ourselves over and over with the same routine—we got away from it all, rejuvenating and replenishing ourselves.

Whatever we do in life starts with us. *To be replenished, we need to keep emptying ourselves to receive more.* In that way, we become vessels, holding up one hand to receive the blessings and then opening up the other hand so that we become channels, letting those blessings flow into the lives of others.

VISION QUEST

If we really want to know ourselves, at some point in life we're going to have to surrender to a Higher Wisdom who knows all about us—our weaknesses, our mistakes, and our potentials. Many Native American tribes do that through our meditation known as the "vision quest"—the setting aside of a time and place, alone out in nature, to communicate with a Higher Being and explore that which is within. Somewhere in that space of time as we are questing, answers come. It's an opportunity to know more about ourselves and some of the options that we have to choose from in life.

Originally, the vision quest was undertaken for the safety of the tribes. Because they lived in a world of upheaval with many wars and battles, young warriors wanting strength and knowledge or leaders seeking guidance and answers would go out alone to fast in the presence of the Great Being. They looked upwards because that's where that Presence seemed to come from. And yet many times it seemed to come from the earth, or it came with the wind, so the Great Presence couldn't be contained in just one area. They didn't have any formal means of praying; they were simply opening themselves to receive. They didn't regard it as prayer; it was a communication. Even today, a vision quest entails many hours of meditation and fasting and doing without everyday comforts as vision questers empty themselves of attachments in order to become ready to receive. And as they fast and wait for communication, they begin to have what is known as *insight.*

One time as I was about to begin a ceremony and was getting my paraphernalia in order, someone came and sat down next to me. After that person got settled he spoke to me: "Hey, brother."

I looked over at him. "Yes?"

"I want you to know I'm going to be in your ceremony and I'm blind."

"Oh, you are?"

"Yes, I'm blind."

"You know, the Creator gave us a beautiful blessing in the form of sight. Many of us can see a beautiful sunset, the stars, and the full moon that lights the night sky. We can see a beautiful picture or read a beautiful verse. But if we don't have sight, He gave us something even more glorious—it's called insight, and even a blind man can have that."

He said, "Thank you, brother."

It's one thing to have sight, but it's a greater gift to have insight into the things that count. That's what our people explored within themselves on a vision quest. They didn't do it through school, they did it with communication. And through that communication they began to understand a little bit more about themselves and their lives.

When I was in my mid-twenties, I vision-quested at Bear Butte in South Dakota. It was my fourth quest and the man who put me up there, a Cheyenne elder, has been gone a long time now. On the third day of my fast, I was sitting in my vision quest site, holding my Pipe in my hand, when a bear came walking up to me. This was not a vision or a dream or hallucination—it was a real, live bear. I laid my Pipe down and the bear stood up. When a bear stands up, he's going to attack. Not wanting a big heavy bear pouncing down on me, I stood up, too, and as I did, he tapped me on my right shoulder. He didn't really strike hard at all, but he was so strong he knocked me down. I got back up and he struck me with the other paw and knocked me down again.

Then I got up and spoke to him in my own language. "My dad was of the Bear Clan, so the bear is my father. I've been told to talk to my father, so I stand here talking to you now. If you want to put your mark on me, go ahead, do whatever satisfies you. I respect you as my father, so I'm not afraid of you. I'm not going to fight you—and I'm not going to run." The bear seemed to listen all that time, then he turned around and walked away.

I went down the mountain and told my sponsor what had happened. He said, "That bear knocked you down twice yet you didn't retaliate. Instead you spoke to him and he listened. When someone has to defend himself, he usually employs force. But instead of defensive actions, it can be better to explain your situation, as you did to the bear—say what you're going to do and what you're not going to do. Come to an understanding and you won't have to use force. Because you stood up to him and didn't run or fight, you showed the spirit and courageous heart of the bear. You have earned the name Bear Heart."

So on that quest, I learned something about myself and my role in life, as well as earned my name.

ON HIGHER GROUND

Our great Native American leaders went on many, many vision quests because each quest is different—we keep adding on, we cannot learn all there is to learn in one shot. When the Great Mystery opens its curtain for just a little peek, there is so much involved we can't contain it all. So we add to what knowledge we have a little at a time through the experiences we have on vision quests.

Today, both men and women vision-quest to receive direction for their lives. They don't go on vision quests to become great leaders, but to take charge of themselves as individuals, so that they can function as a whole in mind, body, and spirit. It's important to function as a complete whole and not leave one part of yourself somewhere else. You may be sitting here but thinking of something five hundred miles away, and that's not functioning as a whole.

A vision quest usually takes place on a high mountain if it's available—that's why we often refer to vision-questing as "going up on the hill." A mountain is preferable, because on a high mountain we have a better perspective of the world in which we live. When we raise our altitude it also raises our attitude because our perspective broadens, not only visually, but inwardly. They go hand in hand. The higher ground seems to give us a sense of the mountain's power and we can receive strength from it, somewhat like feeling the atmosphere of worship in a cathedral or temple. Our faith will become stronger just by being up high. We are not looking down in the sense of being above everything else— it actually makes us more humble to see that we came from below. Being on higher ground seems to create an atmosphere of being close to the Creator—He can come to us more easily. Down below is where most of the activity takes place with other people, so what we're doing is setting ourselves apart from our daily way of living and climbing to a higher place to receive a different kind of communication.

When a mountain isn't available, a vision quest can take place on any piece of land because, according to our elders, wherever we stand—anywhere on this planet—is the center of the universe. And in the center we have the Great Spirit, who can surround us.

When I put someone on a vision quest, they go without food and water for anywhere from one to four days. This is a way of setting aside the daily aspects of life in order to seek communication with a Higher Being. Fasting without food and water is not easy, but if something comes to us easily, where is the glory in victory or achievement? When you have earned something, then you have a good feeling inside because you know you're able to endure. That's why I always say, what is the mark of a good warrior if he has no scars? What battle did he fight? When you see someone all scarred up and still going on, you can say, "That's a good warrior."

So far, I have sent four M.D.s on four-day fasts even though many of their colleagues say no one can survive that long without either food or water. Yet they all survived. In order to receive something, we have to make room for it. If a glass is full of pebbles, it won't hold much water because the rocks take up most of the space. If we have too many attachments, too much activity going on in our lives, very little blessing can come in. By fasting, not only do we empty ourselves physically, but we empty our minds and attitudes to receive new thoughts and concepts. That's what we're doing out there, emptying ourselves to receive communication—to know ourselves better.

KNOWN ONLY TO GOD

On a quest you're searching for something. Some people don't exactly know what their individual role in life is, or perhaps they have tried various avenues that didn't seem to work out. People often seek external means to satisfy an internal questing, but sometimes they can't put their finger on what they are looking for and that brings on an unresolved anxiety, always feeling unfulfilled in everything that they do.

So what do you do when you go on this quest? How do you connect with your inner consciousness? In my tribe, the process of self-knowledge involves asking yourself three questions. The first question is: *Who am I?* In order to succeed in anything, you have to be able to rely upon your own strong identity. With what and with whom do you identify? To find the answer you have to search within. You can never satisfy an internal longing with external means. You have to meet it on its own ground within.

Our elders taught us that someone else can't say, "This is you." You may try to conform to what others think you are, but when all is stripped away, who are you, in actuality? It's important to first identify ourselves, not only in relation to our environment, but in relation to our parents and cultural background. It's very important to know who you are. You may think you know who you are, but perhaps all you are going by is what you do in life because people tend to identify you with your career. You may think that's who you are, but it's not necessarily who you really are inside.

There's a grave in Washington that we call the Tomb of the Unknown Soldier. But the inscription goes on to say, "known only to God." *You have an identity from the One who gave you life. You are known. Search for that path and stay on it.*

You will not have wisdom until you know yourself. What is your character? What do you believe in? What do you stand for? Are you one who is courageous and can bring about change? Or are you of a more gentle and nurturing nature, encouraging those around you on an individual basis? That's why we go out alone on a vision quest—to know ourselves better. I cannot do it for you, no one else can do it for you. Only you can settle once and for all who you are.

Then, after you get that settled, you go on to the next question: *What have I become with the who that I am?*

Someone said a long time ago that when life was given to us it was a gift from the Creator and what we make of that life is our gift back to the Creator. Do you have a mother you honor? Do you have a father you honor? Maybe they're not here anymore, but you can still honor them by the manner in which you live. Are you a role model for someone? If so, what kind of role are you playing in life? Would a little one be proud to follow in your footsteps? What have you become? Have you dragged yourself through many experiences to where you are now? Have you ever considered asking the Creator if you are in the right place and right job? Is there something more that could go along with that? And are you happy in what you are doing? Is this the right road for you, or is it a springboard to greater things yet to come?

In this questing, you determine who you are, and what you have become. Then that leads us to the third question: *Why am I here?* We walk around as human beings, supposedly with a higher intelligence, but is there a purpose for our actions? If we sent out a questionnaire with one question— "What is the purpose of your life?"—the answers would be very interesting. Some people mistake goals as their purpose. A goal can be a means toward a purpose, but is not an end in itself. You may have a goal of becoming a lawyer or doctor, but if you have nothing more in mind, you may not reach the true purpose of your life. If it's in the field of justice, whether it's law enforcement or using the gift of rhetoric in courtroom situations, is it really justice you're after or the big fee that's involved?

There's a reason why you're here, but have you tried to find out what that reason is? Have you fulfilled all of your potential? What motivates you to be what you are? Is it money and accumulation of material rewards, or something else? If you are a cook, you can cook with love and know that the food you prepare is eaten by someone whose life will be extended. If you are a doctor, shopkeeper, lawyer, or carpenter, whatever your career, you have the opportunity to enrich others. Your work can bring you a sense of satisfaction, yet at the same time, you can feel humbled by the fact that you have an opportunity to be of service to others through your chosen field.

Those are the three questions that could occupy your whole time during this quest. You don't have to answer all those questions while you're out there alone, but they may open up some new avenues you haven't considered before about your own life. When you've settled those things for yourself, you more or less know what direction you're headed for in life and will feel more confident. That doesn't mean that your path is going to be easy, but it's going to be worthwhile.

POWER FROM SMALL THINGS

On a vision quest, communication may come to you in dreams or ideas, through a bird, animal, or even a plant. If a bird or animal comes to you on your quest, learn something about it. This is where your powers of observation come into play. What are some of the qualities of that bird or four-legged being? How can you appropriate those qualities for your own life? That animal is a helper designated to assist you, so learn all that you can about it.

When I put someone on a vision quest, they relate to me afterwards all of their experiences—what they saw, the sounds they heard, what they felt or dreamt during this period of time. I interpret all of these things and during that interpretation they may receive answers to some vital questions.

Many people think that they're going to see some kind of an apparition on a vision quest. I once sent on a vision quest a non-Indian who carried a big ledger-type notebook with lots of yellow legal sheets. I guess he was ready for a lot of visions. When he asked if he could take the notebook with him during his fast, I answered, "You might as well. You'll be thinking about it. Might as well take it."

After a few days I brought him back down. He had most of his notebook filled with all kinds of drawings, poetry, and philosophy, but he seemed very disappointed. Apparently he had a preconceived notion that he would see a white buffalo or an eagle or something very dramatic, but all he ended up seeing was one thing: "Right in front of me there was this little patch of grass and no matter where I looked, I always came back to one blade of grass right in the middle of it."

"That's your power symbol."

"What?"

"Your power symbol is a blade of grass. Suppose you had seen an eagle. Compare an eagle feather to this grass. If you were a good marksman with a bow and arrow, you could shoot an eagle feather and break it right in two. If you shoot at a blade of grass, it is so supple it will bend with the force of the arrow and come right back up. The wind may blow hard, but after the wind passes over, the grass will rise again. In all life situations we can learn from our environment, even from a blade of grass. It's teaching you adaptability, to keep getting up in the face of any difficulty.

"Power doesn't always come through great big things. You were looking for a big thing, but there can be big power through a small thing. *We complicate life by thinking that 'my whole life is a big drama' when we were just meant to live a simple life and enjoy it.* Let the small things help to fulfill some of your dreams and your aspirations."

TRAVELING ON THE SMOKE

When people go on a vision quest they need guidance and instruction, they need to know what to look for, so they should have a qualified sponsor to tell them these things. When I sponsor a vision quest, after I have sent all the questers up on the hill, I don't leave the land at all because it is still my responsibility to look after them. There may be anywhere from one to fifteen people fasting at the same time, each in an isolated spot, and I stay in tune with each one who has gone up and I maintain that contact with them in my own way until they come back down.

Before the questers go up to fast, a fire is started for the sweat lodge, and it stays burning at all times—it is the heart of the vision quest and I work with that fire for the protection of the vision questers. In some areas, I have had to keep bears and mountain lions away during the vision quest and many times I have had to keep snakes away, especially the rattlers. If there are rattlesnakes in the area, I shape a snake out of the coals and then I put sweetgrass down and talk to the spirit of the snake, asking it to do no harm to the questers, and I pray for the protection of the snakes as well. If there are other dangerous animals in the area, such as bears or mountain lions, I make a semblance of the shape of that particular animal with the coals and do likewise.

Around ten o'clock at night I fill the Pipe and send the smoke to surround each quester and protect him or her from all harm of any kind—physical, emotional, mental, and spiritual. At midnight I do the same thing, and again at two and at four in the morning. I hardly sleep while each one is up there—I stay up most of each night until the last quester has come down and I have attended to him or her. Often I will get up and smoke before the designated times if I feel someone is in need. I travel psychically on the smoke of the Sacred Pipe and surround people who are up there in order to check on them and see to their safety. If they are in need of help, I will know about it and can take care of them without having to go see them in person.

There are times when a spirit may appear to someone on a vision quest and he or she immediately knows that spirit is quite powerful and that it has something to tell him or her. It may even frighten him or her because of its power. Our bodies are not ready to be on the same plane as the spirits in the spirit world on a regular basis—they exist at a high-velocity vibration and we're not accustomed to it. If the spirits were with us all the time it would make us physically ill. But from time to time we catch glimpses of a spirit and we benefit from its guidance and instructions.

It can't be assumed that all spirits are good, which is why the sponsor must be able to protect each of the vision questers. Some spirit might say, "Hey, come here and take a walk," then lead them to fall over a cliff in the dark or maybe to an animal waiting to pounce. That spirit may be trying to get at the sponsor through them. "Let's see how he'll deal with this. I'll do this to one of the questers and see how powerful his smoke is from down below." When I smoke my Pipe, I pray that no harm of any kind will come to the vision questers. "Surround each one individually and keep them safe. Please be there to give them the strength to know how to face whatever temptations and feelings might come. Let them receive good communication." That's the way my prayers go when I smoke my Pipe.

Then I meet with each person when they come back down and help them to interpret what happened for them, what the lesson is for them in life. These are just some of the things that I do as a sponsor of a vision quest.

I have put two people on a vision quest from a distance while I stayed at home. My belief is such that the power of communication with a Sacred Pipe is not limited by distance. It can still surround them. One girl presented me with to-bacco and I prayed with her, then she went to South Dakota to vision-quest. I stayed in New Mexico and smoked my

Pipe for her as if I was right there and everything went well. She went through some difficult moments, but I was able to explain them to her when she came back and saw me. Afterwards, as is traditional, she gave me a donation.

A year later she decided to vision-quest on her own and went back to South Dakota. She didn't ask me to sponsor her because she felt badly that she had nothing to offer me. If I had known, I would have taken care of her, but she didn't even tell me she was going.

After she completed her vision quest, her totaled-out truck was found near Rapid City. She was in a coma, with her back broken in three places and most of her hair and underlying flesh gone, as if she had been scalped. Although she recovered physically, some of her vision quest is still blanked out by the concussion she experienced. I'm not saying that this will happen to someone without a sponsor, but on a vision quest one is exposed to a variety of entities in such a way that they must have some form of protection. That protection will ensure they experience good communication on the vision quest and not attract anything negative.

The Stillness Within Us

A vision quest is not about looking for a ghost or spirit. By fasting, you become a container, a vessel, emptying yourself to receive communication from a Higher Being who can show you something you can use in your daily life: "That's what I should be doing, this should be my path, this is what will help me."

It's a time of communication to the One Source, and when you return to your daily routine, you can function on the spiritual level as well as in the external world around you.

The survival of our society depends on people who have a good connection with the spiritual. That's our salvation, and without it society deteriorates into politics and greed. We see it almost daily.

If we were to look at the people in the United States, I often wonder how big the spiritual nature would be compared to the population as a whole. It would probably be a little midget within us because we have failed to nurture the spiritual potential within our lives, never feeding or exercising it. Are we truly spiritual, or are we just church members? There's a difference.

So how do we activate this midget within us? By getting away from the hub of all activity that seems to be going nowhere but in circles. *The beauty of silence, the lack of frenzied activity for a period of time helps us collect our thoughts and center our lives so we can maintain a sense of calm when we return to the hectic society and resume our work.* We will be able to cope with life's many challenges by incorporating that stillness into our daily lives. That stillness is actually the presence of the Higher Being, who is with us at all times, even in the busy city. Get away, get in touch once again with what life was supposed to be about, balancing the physical and the spiritual. We have many religions but we have only one spirituality, and that's what we need everywhere. Not only in this country but in the entire world.

You might say, "We're in the 1990s now. Maybe what he's talking about happened way back when the buffalos were roaming along on the plains, but what good will it do in an urban situation? What good is it to receive communication from the Spirit on a vision quest if it's going to leave as soon as I get back to the city limits? What good is all the time and energy spent?"

If that communication is good enough, it's going to stay with you in Los Angeles, New York, or Chicago, even though the attainment of it may require a certain quietness and isolation. Find quiet moments alone, even if it's in the closet or the shower. Try to communicate.

The same Source that was here years ago is still in force with all its power intact. And if that Source can't be present in today's society, then what good is it? The Spirit can be in the business world; it can be in the movie world; it can be anywhere. If you feel that it would be hard to incorporate the traditional values of the Native American into today's society, into what you're doing now, then you're saying something must be wrong with the Spirit. Whether you're an executive in an office building or a nurse in the emergency room, the Spirit is there.

16

WE ALL HAVE
SOMETHING TO OFFER

I REMEMBER ONE OF MY ELDERS TELLING ME, "CHEBON, everything has a purpose. See that butterfly? Pretty soon it will fly off, but it's not flying just because it has wings. It has a destination. That grasshopper over there will sit awhile and then it's going to hop away. There's a reason for that. Everything has a purpose and a reason, always remember that. As you go through life, go with a purpose in mind, don't just wander around like a tumbleweed."

We have many tumbleweeds in New Mexico going where the wind blows. Sometimes keeping your purpose means walking against the wind to reach your destination.

In the movie *Dances With Wolves*, a young man from the East volunteers to go to the West because he wants to see the western frontier and have new experiences. Searching, searching, searching. He finds a mate, but most important of all, he finds himself. The final key to the whole story is at the end—no longer the person he was, now he is Dances With Wolves, fully accepted by the Lakota tribe and himself.

Finding yourself, looking within, is the most important thing in life. "This is where I stand. This is who I am." When you know that, you can tackle any circumstance that comes along.

You're glad that you are you, regardless of what other people might say. Maybe your own parents discouraged you from your childhood dreams and aspirations, or some friends said, "I don't think you ought to do this." What do they know? They're not living your life. It's you who has to live with yourself. What you find good within yourself, that's what's most important. If you are in harmony with yourself, with your mind, your body, and your soul, then what else is there? There's nothing that cannot be overcome.

Someone once said to me, "I wish I had the same amount of spirit that you have." I turned to him and said, "We were all given the same amount of spirit. None more, none less. The difference between individuals is allowing the Spirit to have more of you." So that's where the difference is, yielding to that spirit more. Although you seemingly have yielded, you may still be holding back in many ways.

Whether it's through a vision quest or through introspection and contemplation, opening yourself to receive direction from a Higher Intelligence is known as the inner quest—searching within, trying to bring out the real you, including your emotions and beliefs. There is a path for each of us to follow—that's what life is all about. *Many people say to me, "I'd like to learn your ways." That's okay with me, but I would rather have people learn their own way, and equally important is how they use what they learn.*

QUEST FOR WISDOM

"Questing" is something all people have done from childhood. You have quested for knowledge ever since preschool and kindergarten, on up through the university. Traditionally, the Creek people's primary focus wasn't on how smart we became. Our focus was on wisdom—how we used what little we had.

I've always enjoyed the story about the man whose tire fell off his car right in front of a mental institution. Apparently someone didn't tighten the lugs properly after fixing his tire, so it came off and the car fell onto the axle. He had a heck of a time raising the car with his jack to the proper level, but he finally did, retrieved the tire and put it on, but all the lugs were missing and he didn't know how to secure it.

An inmate was watching all this from behind the fence and shouted out, "Hey, mister! You want me to tell you how to keep that tire on until you can get to a service station?"

This man was already hot, bothered, tired, and disgusted. "You?"

"Yes, me."

"All right. Tell me."

"Take one lug from each of the other wheels. Put them on that tire and it will stay on until you get to where you're going. I may be crazy, but I'm not stupid."

You can be a double Ph.D. in any given course, but if you don't have wisdom to go along with that knowledge, then you can get into trouble. I sometimes speak to the inmates of various penal institutions and there are many Ph.D.s there—they had knowledge, but they didn't have the wisdom to use that knowledge in the right way. We learn many things as we grow up. But how do we use them? That's where wisdom comes in—wisdom to guide that knowledge.

My grandson, Bobby, was six-foot-two and weighed 180 pounds at thirteen years old. One day he was standing in line to pay for lunch at school and his friend standing next to him took out his money. Playfully, Bobby took the money, just to tease him, and then someone behind him took the money from him. It went on down the lunch line, and by the time it got back to his friend, part of that money was missing. The principal got involved and called Bobby's mother at work because Bobby wouldn't tell who actually got the money. He really wasn't sure who had it. His mother grounded him—no more Nintendo, no more bringing home friends, no more overnights with friends until you resolve this with the school.

My grandson wants to follow in my footsteps for whatever reasons. I haven't told him he ought to do this, he wants to do it, to learn some of my ways, and I've had long talks with him about dealing with various situations. He was grounded and deprived of certain privileges, but he didn't say anything. He wanted to be true to his friend, but he didn't want to snitch on the others, either, so he was caught in the middle.

The next day he went to school and came back as if nothing happened. His mother said, "Well, how did it go?"

"Okay."

"What do you mean, 'okay'?"

"Two boys admitted to the principal that they took the money."

"How is it that they admitted they're the ones who took it?"

He just nonchalantly said, "I told them to."

That's all it took for him to settle the situation. At thirteen years old he was beginning to use a little wisdom.

So wisdom is something to look for—a quest. The beginning of wisdom for each one of us is to understand ourselves a little better. Strive to find your true identity, your role in life, your potential, and your limitations. Once you are aware of these things, then you have something to work with in order to grow.

GOING BEYOND THE WALLS

There was a man in the Bible by the name of Jacob, and one of the greatest wrestling matches ever recorded was when he wrestled an angel because he wanted a blessing. He got his hip thrown out of joint, but he wouldn't give up. He kept wrestling until he got the blessing. Jacob received this blessing because of his perseverance, his unwillingness to give up in spite of physical injury to himself. By that same token, whatever we want in life is possible for us to achieve, although the attainment of it may not be easy. If it's a worthwhile goal, it keeps us going forward. *Too often we define success in terms of financial achievement. I view success as doing your very best at all costs.*

Abraham Lincoln suffered many defeats in politics before he ever became president of the United States. He was laughed at because he was ugly. Someone once told him he looked like an ape, but when Lincoln got to be president, he appointed that person to his cabinet because he was the most qualified. Lincoln had the ability to overlook those little slurs and slights, accepting them. We hear of blind poets and deaf composers; it's hard to imagine, yet they still wrote and composed because they had something within them that said they could do it. It shows us that if you want something badly enough and strive for it, you can do it. It may not come overnight, but your persistence will win out.

We view much of life around us from our own little safety perch. We look and say, "How I wish I could be that. How I wish I could do that." Regardless of what field you go into, there's going to be someone who's a little better at it. But what of it? If someone can do better, wonderful for them, but there are some things you are better at than that one. Always remember that, don't focus on the other person who can do one thing better than you. Maybe you can do two things better than the other person can. It balances out. You have it within you to become good at anything you strive for. The thing is, never give up, accept what you are and be proud of it, be grateful for it. But never let it go to your head, always keep your feet on the ground.

We strive to meet goals, but in our plans, we should see beyond the goal. Once we have achieved that goal, what are we going to do with it? The goal was merely a starting point. Once achieved, a new plan comes into play and we begin to expand from that point into other fields.

When I was living in Oklahoma, I visited many different penal institutions and spoke to the Indian inmates. I know that many Indians are very talented, so on one of my visits to a group at Stringtown, I told them, "I'm not here trying to make you think that I'm better than any of you. We are all alike, we are all one. Not only in color and race, but in our heritage. And I'm not here to judge and say someone has done wrong, or point my finger saying you're guilty of this and you're guilty of that. I'm here to recognize each one of you as an individual human being. Even though your freedom is limited, there are some things that no bars or doors or fences can ever contain and that's freedom of thought. You can have aspirations, dreams, and visions. There are things that you can still do, even in a limited space. Many of you are poets. Many of you are artists. Why don't you put your talents together, contact a group of businessmen, and find an outlet for your work? Those are just some of the ways in which your mind can go beyond these walls."

After I spoke to them they gathered some art supplies and went to work. Some were very good artists and they got the Chamber of Commerce of a nearby town to sell their art and they collected money over several months. At the end of the school year, they chose one Indian preschool and they paid for those Indian children and their parents to go to Disneyland in California.

So they found freedom in a limited space and did something about it. *Just because you fall off a horse, you don't have to lie there.* If all you can do is crawl, then crawl. If you can get up, walk. If you have to limp, find something to lean on and keep going. Never say, "This is it," and give up. Think about the thrill those children received on the rides at Disneyland, seeing some of the characters they'd read about. How do you put a price tag on the joy that a little child receives? And what did it do for the inmates?

Suppose you see two people working and ask, "What are you doing?" One would proudly say, "I'm making twelve fifty an hour." And you turn to the other one. "What are you doing?" "I'm building a church." He had the same job with the same amount of pay, but the motivation, the feeling is different when you know you're working to help others. Then it becomes something very significant. That project was healing for the inmates. Instead of putting them through a counseling program, all they needed was a little encouragement—"You have it within you to do something constructive." And they did. It made me very proud of them.

Each one of us has something to offer in this life, every one of us. I don't care about your background, what your academic standing is. You may have a double Ph.D., or maybe you never got more than a D in school. You have something to give. All of us have something to contribute.

When the railroads were active, way back before Amtrak, we had the Chieftain, the New York Central, and the Baltimore and Ohio. I used to ride all of them. There was a railroad employee who had a shift requiring him to be away from home for days at a time. His family lived in a company house along the railroad track. The front yard had no lawn, just dirt, and in the back of the house was a field. He had three children—a boy and girl and a four-year-old who was slightly retarded and could not walk. He had to crawl wherever he went.

On the days that their father was to be coming home, the children used to look down the railroad track and watch for him: "Daddy will be coming home soon." And sure enough, he would be walking home carrying his coat and his lunch bucket. That was the cue for the two older children to go out back to pick wildflowers and make little bouquets. As their father came closer they would run to meet him. "Dad, I made this bouquet for you." He would take both in his arms, kiss them, and carry them back home. It was a beautiful sight.

What about the little one? He couldn't run out and pick beautiful flowers. He couldn't walk. So, as far as he could reach in that dirt yard, he'd pick up a little rock. No particular rock, just any ordinary rock and a little stick over here. He'd have a few little rocks and sticks in his hands and when Dad came into that yard he called out, "Dada, Dada!" He wanted to make a presentation, too.

So that's why I say it doesn't matter what station in life you happen to represent, you have something to offer. And the opportunity to offer it is today, not ten years from now.

We are here to reflect the beauty of all of life—the beauty of the trees, the grass, the animals, the birds, the rivers as they flow by. All these may be lost in time. While we are still here, can we not appreciate and love the land, the environment, so that when we pass on, we will have left something solid and beautiful for those who are going to follow after us? Are those of us here now building a solid foundation on which our young people can grow strong and be productive in a positive way?

Perhaps one of the greatest ways we can teach is to live by example, showing our young ones what we want them to learn. Our actions speak for themselves. Instead of pointing a finger and saying, "I don't know what's become of those youngsters," we should look at ourselves. When we die, the grandchildren we leave behind may grow up and become sickly because of the pollution that we caused. When their friends are shot down for no reason at all, they'll ask, "Why couldn't they stop the gangs, the drive-by shootings?"

There was a time when the Indian people never heard of suicide. It was a rare, rare occurrence. Then they left the reservations and their traditions, went into urban areas, and the children got exposed to cutting classes in school, partying, and smoking pot. Maybe in this competitive world both parents are working and there is a lot of unsupervised time for the kids. Young people get hooked on drugs they can't afford to buy over and over unless they have a decent job, and they can't hold a decent job if they're doing all this stuff. It gets too big to cope with, so we had a lot of young Indian people committing suicide because they lost touch with their roots and their purpose.

Bring it down to 1994 in Albuquerque, a sixteen-year-old

and two other teenagers killed his grandparents because the grandparents didn't want them drinking beer in their home. I'm talking about values in life—where do we get them? Go back to the basics. In our ceremonies, we try to find out what it takes to put meaning into life. How we can apply ourselves in a constructive manner—this is what needs to be presented to schoolchildren today.

Our elders taught that when you shoot an arrow, you first have to pull it back before it can go forward. That was the basis of our greatest teaching—self-knowledge. Before you can progress, know who you are, know those things that you don't like about yourself, then know your potential. From there you can go forward. Our children were first taught to shoot an arrow as far as they could. Then, after they had learned that, they were taught direction and how to hit a target. So after you have learned something about yourself, self-discipline is the next step. We have many ways of learning to live in harmony with our environment, but first we must learn to live in harmony with ourselves. If we can't master ourselves, how can we master anything else?

Questing to know ourselves teaches us how to live before we spend too much time in learning to make a living. If we leave out that "how to live," we may be able to make a living, but what if the stock market drops suddenly, or our source of income is cut off? If we don't know how to live, we may hit bottom when those external things we rely on are gone. But if we learn how to live, in spite of setbacks, we will continue on, we can find avenues to sustain us and life will be meaningful for us. This is why I'd like for young people today to learn about some of our traditions because they are tools to live by, ways that bring meaning into life.

THE GIVEAWAY

Most people have heard the expression "Indian giver" as meaning giving something and then taking it right back. That was a misinterpretation that got started a long time ago. As poor as we are, Native American people are known for their generosity. I said earlier that it is hard for us to say thank you with nothing in our hand—giving is integral to our way of life.

The true tradition of the "giveaway" is to show appreciation by giving out a few gifts. At a gathering such as a pow-wow, someone may call your name and give you a gift, perhaps a blanket, or even money. You may have been in great need at that time and you never forgot, so three or four years later at another big gathering, you call that person up—it's your turn now. You tell him, "So many years ago you filled my heart with joy. I've never forgotten it. To show that I've been thinking about you, I got this especially for you and I want you to have it." And you give that person a gift—it's our way of saying thank you. True Indian giving is when someone gives you something and later on you give that person something in return. They're getting something back, but not the same object.

The giveaway tradition started out in some of our funeral services, when we were putting away our loved ones. There would be a great feast, and the family was glad that so many people had come to honor their loved one, so they could be put away with dignity. They'd call someone up and maybe give that person a blanket or a shawl. *What they were doing was this—when you make someone happy, he will take some of that hurt that you're feeling, take it far enough away to where the winds will catch it.* It makes your own hurt a little easier, a little lighter. You give away from your heart and you give away on behalf of your loved one. That's how most of our giveaways got started. Then the practice was extended into a form of appreciation. So that is the tradition of our giveaway.

I Called You "Brother"

In our Indian tradition, we also have "adoption." I have many adopted relatives, from many tribes. One is Raymond Butler of the Otoe tribe in Oklahoma—he's my brother by adoption. A few months after my son's death, Raymond held a big feast for me and my family. After we got through eating, he stood up and said, "Brother, you helped to put my mother away when she passed on and you said some beautiful words that I never forgot. I called you 'brother' at that time and we've become real close. You haven't helped only my family. Our entire tribe hears about how you help other people. When they're crying, you go over there and always seem to look after them. Now it has come to the point where you yourself shed tears over your great loss. There's nothing we can do for you. I wish we could. But my wife and I called you here because we want to share our oldest son with you so that you can have someone you can call 'Son.' And he can call you 'Dad.'" Then he put a blanket around me and put some money in my hands. That's our way of adoption.

So it became that way. From that time on, Bubby Butler was like a real son to me. Every Father's Day I'd get a card from him, maybe something in the way of a package. It was a beautiful relationship, just like with a birth son. I'd come and bless his children and he'd take care of the drum when

I ran tipi meetings. He was a very good drummer. He knew my songs, and when I handled so many meetings that my throat was getting a little husky, he'd carry on and sing those songs for me.

Bubby was the head of the HUD program for the tribe. He had to evict two families after many notices because his supervisors said, "You have to do this." In retaliation, the families had been harassing him all summer long. On one particular night, he was sponsoring a tipi meeting for his own son's fifteenth birthday. Everything was going real fine. Bubby was taking care of the drum and he had a Cheyenne brother conducting the meeting for him.

'Round about midnight young boys from those families came around the meeting, harassing people and throwing beer cans at the tipi. They started cutting that brand-new tipi with a knife. It was a meeting for his son, his place, so Bubby felt the responsibility and ran out to see about it. That's what the boys wanted. They ganged up on him and one stabbed him in the back. When he fell to the ground, they stomped his face in and killed him.

Those who were in the tipi came out and found his body on the ground. When they picked him up, he still had that drumstick in his hand—a badge of his faith in a living God and his loyalty even unto death.

My grandson has a hard time whenever his birthday comes around because he thinks of his dad, who went on. There are many, many people I have attended from all walks of life, people who've been hurt in some way or other, and I try to make things right, but the greatest challenge that was ever presented to me as a medicine person, as well as a human being, was when I heard about my adopted son's murder. How does one deal with something like that? I had the power to do something very bad to each one of those boys, even at a distance. But by so doing I would be no better than the ones who took the life of my son.

I have a Sacred Pipe that does not allow me to use it for revenge. I must fill it and let Him take care of things like that. I really had to pray about it. I told the Great Being, "I cannot condone what they did, but those boys are still Your creation and if I talk about love I have to love all mankind, from all walks of life. And You see my situation, because I loved my son and I'm taking this personally. I want to love these people in Your way, but I can't. So I'm asking that You continue to love them through me so I will understand how Your love works—not something we just talk about but something that we can experience and live."

I went from New Mexico to Oklahoma and handled the whole burial ceremony. Among the Otoe tribe, the dead are buried on the fourth day. Until then, speeches are made every night and I had to give the main speech to a whole group of people in a gymnasium where the casket lay. After all the people had crowded in, it was my turn to speak about the son that he was to me.

I told the people, "Within the life of my son there was a soul. There is no knife long enough to have touched that soul—it's still intact. His body was destroyed, but it was merely a housing for the soul that lives on. For that part, I'm confident that he's all right. When you take something away, in simple arithmetic, we call it subtraction. A minus sign that's represented by a horizontal bar. Taking away. That's what those young boys tried to do—take away his life.

"My son was taking care of the sacred drum. When they picked his body up, he still had that drumstick in his hand. Faithful and loyal even unto death, that drumstick indicated his own belief in a Higher Being, from his heart to the heart of the Creator. That makes a vertical, and it makes a plus out of that minus sign."

If you have a negative, if you have a minus sign in your life, think of the story I just related. If a young Indian from the Otoe reservation at Red Rock, Oklahoma, could die for his belief, could die for his faith, could die for the hope of good things for his own son and his family, what you and I can do now is live for something. Live for our beliefs, live our faith. Live for the hope of good things to come, not only here and now, but in generations to follow.

The word *memorial* does not indicate that someone has died. It symbolizes that someone has lived. What is going to be that living memorial that you're going to leave behind? That I'm going to leave behind? Why are we here now? We're here to add something, to construct, to preserve. To leave something good for those little ones who are going to come into our world. Let that motivation be so firmly established in your heart and mind that you can say, "I will stand for this. I will live for this."

PRAYERS

Morning Prayer
"I thank You for another day. I ask that You give me the strength to walk worthily this day so that when I lie down at night I will not be ashamed."

Evening Prayer
At the end of each day, face west and say: "Thank you for all the things that happened today, the good as well as the bad."

For Emotional, Physical, and Mental Health
Lie down with your navel toward the Earth and your head to the north, saying: "Grandmother Earth, please send your healing energy through this body and bring it back into balance."

To Find an Answer to a Problem
Face east and think about your problem, saying: "Grandfather Sun, you come each day to dispel the darkness. In that same way I ask you to shed your light so that I may see where to take the next step."

If You Have Lost a Loved One
Facing south, say: "Help me to know my loved one is with the Great Spirit and has found rest and peace. One day we will be reunited, but until then I ask for help to keep going on in life."